Finding Peace in Your Life and in This World

By DBUGKING

In the tumultuous tapestry of life, where chaos often seems to reign, the quest for peace becomes a beacon illuminating our journey. *Finding Peace in Your Life and in This World* embarks on a profound exploration into the essence of peace, both within the individual soul and across the interconnected web of humanity. As we navigate the complexities of our existence, the pursuit of peace emerges not only as a personal aspiration but as an urgent and collective necessity for our shared global landscape.

In the opening chapters of this book, we delve into the multifaceted dimensions of peace, from its ethereal presence in ancient wisdom traditions to its tangible manifestation in modern psychological and philosophical approaches. As we traverse the internal realms of the mind and spirit, we uncover the transformative power of mindfulness, meditation, and cognitive behavioral therapy. Through the lenses of spiritual and philosophical perspectives, we draw inspiration from the timeless teachings of traditions such as Buddhism, Taoism, and Stoicism, seeking to distill their wisdom into practical guidance for the modern seeker.

The narrative then seamlessly transitions to the external facets of peace, exploring the intricate dance of interpersonal relationships and the broader canvas of global harmony. Communication strategies, forgiveness, conflict resolution, and the intersection of human rights and social justice are unraveled, offering insights and tools to foster peace in our everyday interactions and on the world stage.

With a keen eye on practical applications, this book equips readers with tools drawn from mind-body practices like yoga and tai chi, emphasizing the connection between physical well-being and inner tranquility. We illuminate the profound impact of community engagement, volunteering, and acts of kindness on personal and collective peace, underscoring the transformative potential embedded in seemingly simple actions.

As we navigate this exploration, the pages come alive with stories of resilience, triumph, and the indomitable human spirit's capacity to find peace amidst life's storms. Through meticulously researched insights, expert opinions, and real-life examples, *Finding Peace in Your Life and in This World* seeks not only to inform but to inspire and guide you on your personal journey toward a more peaceful existence.

This book is more than a compilation of knowledge; it is a roadmap, a companion, and a testament to the possibility of finding peace—within yourself and in the world that surrounds you. Join us on this transformative odyssey, as together, we navigate the path to serenity and contribute to the collective tapestry of global peace.

Table of Contents

Chapter I: Definition of Peace

Introduction: Peace, a word with profound significance, stands as both an aspiration and a reality, shaping the human experience in myriad ways. In the opening chapter of *Finding Peace in Your Life and in This World*, we embark on a nuanced exploration of the multifaceted nature of peace. Beyond the absence of conflict, peace is a dynamic force, weaving through the fabric of personal well-being and global harmony. This chapter aims to define peace in its various dimensions, offering a foundation for the journey ahead.

Inner Peace:

A. Psychological Perspectives:

Exploration of Inner Peace from a Psychological Standpoint

1 Understanding the Psychological Landscape:

Definition of Inner Peace: **1. Psychological Perspectives on Inner Peace:**

- **Cognitive Perspective:**
    - Definition: Inner peace is a cognitive state characterized by cognitive harmony and equilibrium.
    - Framework: Investigating how cognitive restructuring and positive thinking contribute to inner peace.
- **Emotional Perspective:**
    - Definition: Inner peace is emotional resilience and the ability to navigate emotions effectively.
    - Framework: Examining emotion regulation strategies and their role in achieving and maintaining inner peace.
- **Existential Perspective:**
    - Definition: Inner peace is a sense of existential fulfillment and alignment with one's purpose.
    - Framework: Exploring existential psychology and its implications for finding peace in life.

2. Mindfulness-Based Definitions:

- **Mindfulness-Based Stress Reduction (MBSR):**
    - Definition: Inner peace is a natural byproduct of mindfulness practices.
    - Framework: Investigating Jon Kabat-Zinn's MBSR program and its impact on psychological well-being.
- **Mindfulness-Based Cognitive Therapy (MBCT):**
    - Definition: Inner peace through the integration of mindfulness and cognitive-behavioral approaches.

    o Framework: Examining how MBCT addresses recurrent thought patterns and promotes peace of mind.

3. Positive Psychology Perspectives:

- **Subjective Well-Being:**
  - o Definition: Inner peace as a component of subjective well-being.
  - o Framework: Exploring positive psychology interventions that enhance life satisfaction and contribute to inner peace.
- **Flow State:**
  - o Definition: Inner peace is a state of "flow" characterized by complete immersion and focus.
  - o Framework: Investigating Mihaly Csikszentmihalyi's concept of flow and its psychological implications.

4. Integrative Approaches:

- **Holistic Psychology:**
  - o Definition: Inner peace is a holistic integration of mind, body, and spirit.
  - o Framework: Examining approaches that emphasize the interconnectedness of psychological, physical, and spiritual well-being.
- **Ecopsychology:**
  - o Definition: Inner peace in connection with the natural world.
  - o Framework: Exploring the psychological benefits of nature-based interventions in promoting inner peace.

Key Insights:

- Inner peace is viewed through various psychological lenses, encompassing cognitive, emotional, existential, and mindfulness-based perspectives.
- Positive psychology offers insights into subjective well-being and the promotion of inner peace through interventions.
- Integrative approaches emphasize the importance of considering the interconnected aspects of psychological well-being for achieving lasting inner peace.

This examination provides a comprehensive overview of the diverse psychological definitions and frameworks surrounding inner peace, laying the groundwork for a nuanced understanding of this complex and multifaceted concept.

Defining Markers of Mental and Emotional Tranquility

1. Emotional Stability:

- **Consistent Mood:**
  - o Marker: Emotional states that remain relatively stable over time.

- o Explanation: Examining the ability to maintain a consistent emotional baseline without extreme fluctuations.
- **Resilience in the Face of Challenges:**
  - o Marker: The capacity to bounce back emotionally after facing adversity.
  - o Explanation: Identifying how individuals handle stress and setbacks without a prolonged negative impact on their emotional well-being.

2. Cognitive Harmony:

- **Clarity of Thought:**
  - o Marker: A clear and focused thought process.
  - o Explanation: Investigating how mental clarity contributes to a sense of tranquility and the ability to make sound decisions.
- **Effective Problem-Solving:**
  - o Marker: The ability to approach challenges with a calm and rational mindset.
  - o Explanation: Understanding how mental tranquility enhances problem-solving skills and decision-making processes.

3. Self-Awareness and Mindfulness:

- **Emotional Awareness:**
  - o Marker: A heightened awareness of one's own emotions.
  - o Explanation: Exploring the role of emotional intelligence and self-awareness in achieving emotional tranquility.
- **Mindful Presence:**
  - o Marker: The ability to be fully present in the current moment.
  - o Explanation: Examining mindfulness as a practice that fosters mental tranquility by reducing rumination and promoting presence.

4. Healthy Coping Mechanisms:

- **Adaptive Coping Strategies:**
  - o Marker: Engaging in constructive coping mechanisms in response to stress.
  - o Explanation: Identifying healthy strategies for managing stress and adversity without resorting to harmful behaviors.
- **Effective Stress Management:**
  - o Marker: Utilizing stress management techniques to maintain emotional balance.
  - o Explanation: Investigating how individuals cope with stressors to prevent the accumulation of emotional tension.

5. Interpersonal Relationships:

- **Positive Social Connections:**
  - o Marker: Nurturing positive and supportive relationships.
  - o Explanation: Understanding the impact of healthy social connections on mental and emotional well-being.

- **Empathy and Emotional Regulation in Relationships:**
  - o Marker: The ability to empathize and regulate emotions within interpersonal dynamics.
  - o Explanation: Exploring the role of emotional intelligence in maintaining harmonious relationships.

Key Insights:

- Markers of mental and emotional tranquility include emotional stability, cognitive harmony, self-awareness, mindfulness, healthy coping mechanisms, and positive interpersonal relationships.
- Achieving emotional tranquility involves not only managing emotions but also developing resilience, self-awareness, and effective coping strategies.
- The interconnectedness of emotional and mental well-being highlights the importance of a holistic approach to achieving a state of tranquility.

This exploration of markers provides a framework for understanding the components that contribute to mental and emotional tranquility, forming the basis for further discussions on cultivating inner peace.

1. Mindfulness and Meditation

Defining Mindfulness: Cultivating Present-Moment Awareness

1. Foundations of Mindfulness:

- **Rooted in Ancient Wisdom:**
  - o Tracing mindfulness to its origins in ancient contemplative traditions, particularly within Buddhism.
  - o Highlighting its adaptation and integration into secular contexts in contemporary settings.

2. Core Element: Present-Moment Awareness:

- **Definition:**
  - o Mindfulness as the intentional cultivation of present-moment awareness.
  - o Emphasizing a non-judgmental and accepting attitude toward one's thoughts, feelings, and sensations.
- **Anchoring to the Now:**
  - o Exploring the concept of "being in the moment" and the significance of anchoring attention to the present.
  - o Discussing the contrast with mind-wandering and the impact on overall well-being.

3. Mindful Observation:

- **Observing Thoughts and Sensations:**

- o Encouraging individuals to observe their thoughts, emotions, and bodily sensations without attachment or aversion.
    - o Illustrating how mindfulness involves stepping back to become an impartial observer of one's internal experiences.
- **Cultivating a Witnessing Presence:**
    - o Describing the development of a witnessing presence that allows for greater clarity and understanding of the present moment.
    - o Recognizing the impermanent nature of thoughts and sensations.

4. Breath as an Anchor:

- **Focus on the Breath:**
    - o Presenting the breath as a common focal point in mindfulness practices.
    - o Exploring how conscious breathing serves as an anchor to the present moment.
- **Connection to Body Sensations:**
    - o Discussing the embodiment of mindfulness through the awareness of breath-related sensations in the body.
    - o Highlighting the somatic aspect of present-moment awareness.

5. Non-Judgmental Acceptance:

- **Acceptance of What Is:**
    - o Emphasizing the practice of non-judgmental acceptance of thoughts and emotions.
    - o Encouraging individuals to acknowledge experiences without labeling them as good or bad.
- **Compassionate Self-Observation:**
    - o Introducing the concept of self-compassion in mindfulness.
    - o Encouraging a kind and gentle approach to self-observation.

6. Integration into Daily Life:

- **Mindfulness Beyond Formal Practice:**
    - o Discussing the integration of mindfulness into daily activities.
    - o Highlighting the potential for cultivating present-moment awareness in routine tasks.
- **Mindful Eating, Walking, and Listening:**
    - o Illustrating how mindfulness can be applied to activities such as eating, walking, and listening, enhancing the richness of these experiences.

7. Conclusion:

- **Summarizing Mindfulness:**
    - o Defining mindfulness as a transformative practice rooted in cultivating present-moment awareness.
    - o Emphasizing its potential to foster a deep connection with the unfolding reality of each moment.

This definition serves as a foundation for understanding mindfulness, providing a clear framework for its practice and its profound implications for mental, emotional, and physical well-being.

Tracing the Origins of Mindfulness to Ancient Contemplative Traditions, particularly within Buddhism

1. Buddhist Roots of Mindfulness:

- **Historical Context:**
    - Exploring the historical origins of mindfulness within the Buddhist tradition.
    - Noting its emergence in the teachings of Siddhartha Gautama, the historical Buddha, over 2,500 years ago.

2. Pali Canon and Satipatthana Sutta:

- **Foundational Texts:**
    - Discussing the significance of the Pali Canon, the earliest collection of Buddhist scriptures.
    - Highlighting the Satipatthana Sutta as a key discourse where mindfulness is expounded by the Buddha.
- **Four Foundations of Mindfulness:**
    - Identifying the Satipatthana Sutta's delineation of mindfulness in the context of four foundations: body, feelings, mind, and mental qualities.

3. Buddhist Meditation Practices:

- **Vipassana Meditation:**
    - Exploring Vipassana meditation as a central Buddhist practice for cultivating insight through mindfulness.
    - Describing the focus on observing sensations in the body to develop heightened awareness.
- **Zen and Mindfulness:**
    - Investigating the integration of mindfulness within Zen Buddhism.
    - Discussing the emphasis on present-moment awareness in Zen meditation (zazen).

4. Mindfulness Beyond Buddhism:

- **Spread to Contemplative Traditions:**
    - Tracing the dissemination of mindfulness practices to other contemplative traditions beyond Buddhism.
    - Acknowledging the influence on Hinduism, Taoism, and various forms of Christian mysticism.

5. Introduction to the West:

- **Thich Nhat Hanh and Mindfulness in the West:**
  - o Highlighting the role of influential figures like Thich Nhat Hanh in introducing mindfulness to the Western world.
  - o Discussing the integration of mindfulness into secular contexts.
- **MBSR and Jon Kabat-Zinn:**
  - o Exploring the development of Mindfulness-Based Stress Reduction (MBSR) by Jon Kabat-Zinn.
  - o Recognizing the secular adaptation of mindfulness for health and well-being.

6. Scientific Exploration of Mindfulness:

- **Mindfulness in Research:**
  - o Noting the surge in scientific research on mindfulness, examining its psychological and physiological effects.
  - o Discussing how these studies have contributed to the widespread acceptance of mindfulness in contemporary contexts.

7. Conclusion:

- **Legacy of Ancient Wisdom:**
  - o Emphasizing the enduring legacy of mindfulness from its roots in ancient contemplative traditions.
  - o Recognizing its adaptability and relevance in diverse cultural and spiritual landscapes.

This exploration traces the rich history of mindfulness, acknowledging its profound roots in ancient Buddhist contemplative traditions and its evolution into a globally recognized practice for well-being and self-awareness.

Expert Opinions on Mindfulness from Psychologists and Practitioners

1. Psychological Perspectives:

- **Dr. Ellen Langer, Harvard University:**
  - o *Expert Opinion:* Dr. Langer emphasizes mindfulness as a key factor in promoting psychological well-being. She explores the concept of "mindful learning" and its impact on cognitive processes, decision-making, and overall mental health.
- **Dr. Jon Kabat-Zinn, Mindfulness Pioneer:**
  - o *Expert Opinion:* As the founder of Mindfulness-Based Stress Reduction (MBSR), Dr. Kabat-Zinn provides insights into the transformative power of mindfulness in reducing stress and enhancing emotional resilience. His work highlights the intersection of psychology and contemplative practices.

2. Mindfulness Practitioners:

- **Thich Nhat Hanh, Zen Master:**

- *Practitioner's Insight:* Thich Nhat Hanh shares wisdom on mindfulness as a path to inner peace and global harmony. His teachings emphasize the integration of mindfulness into daily life, fostering compassion and understanding.
- **Sharon Salzberg, Meditation Teacher:**
  - *Practitioner's Insight:* Sharon Salzberg, a prominent meditation teacher, offers practical perspectives on mindfulness and its role in cultivating loving-kindness. She discusses the psychological benefits of meditation and the importance of self-compassion.

3. Clinical Psychologists:

- **Dr. Tara Brach, Clinical Psychologist:**
  - *Expert Opinion:* Dr. Brach integrates mindfulness into psychotherapy and explores its role in cultivating emotional healing. Her work emphasizes the importance of self-compassion and mindfulness in overcoming emotional challenges.
- **Dr. Mark Williams, University of Oxford:**
  - *Expert Opinion:* Dr. Williams, a pioneer in mindfulness-based cognitive therapy (MBCT), provides insights into the application of mindfulness in preventing relapse for individuals with recurrent depression. His work highlights the psychological mechanisms underlying mindfulness interventions.

4. Neuroscientists:

- **Dr. Richard Davidson, Center for Healthy Minds:**
  - *Expert Opinion:* Dr. Davidson's research delves into the neuroscience of mindfulness. He discusses how mindfulness practices can reshape the brain, fostering emotional resilience and well-being.
- **Dr. Sara Lazar, Harvard Medical School:**
  - *Expert Opinion:* Dr. Lazar's neuroscientific studies focus on the impact of mindfulness on brain structures. Her work highlights the positive neurological changes associated with regular mindfulness practice.

5. Integration of Mindfulness in Clinical Settings:

- **Dr. Zindel Segal, University of Toronto:**
  - *Expert Opinion:* Dr. Segal's expertise lies in the clinical application of mindfulness, particularly in preventing relapse in individuals with depression. His insights offer a bridge between psychological research and therapeutic practice.
- **Dr. Shauna Shapiro, Santa Clara University:**
  - *Expert Opinion:* Dr. Shapiro explores the intersection of mindfulness and positive psychology. Her work emphasizes the cultivation of mindfulness for increased well-being and resilience.

6. Conclusion:

- Bringing together expert opinions from psychologists and mindfulness practitioners provides a holistic understanding of mindfulness's impact on mental health. These perspectives contribute to the ongoing dialogue surrounding the integration of mindfulness into psychological theory and clinical practice.

meditation is a practice that involves training your mind to focus and redirect thoughts. There are various meditation techniques, and here are some basic ones to get you started:

1. Mindfulness Meditation:

- *Purpose:* Cultivating present-moment awareness.
- *Technique:*
    1. Find a quiet and comfortable place to sit or lie down.
    2. Close your eyes and bring attention to your breath.
    3. Notice each inhale and exhale, paying attention to the sensations and the rhythm.
    4. When your mind wanders (and it will), gently bring it back to your breath without judgment.

2. Guided Meditation:

- *Purpose:* Following a guided script or recording.
- *Technique:*
    1. Use guided meditation apps, recordings, or live sessions.
    2. Follow the instructions provided by the guide.
    3. Typically, this involves visualizing peaceful scenes, focusing on the breath, or body scan techniques.

3. Body Scan Meditation:

- *Purpose:* Increasing awareness of bodily sensations and promoting relaxation.
- *Technique:*
    1. Lie down or sit comfortably.
    2. Direct your focus to different parts of your body, starting from toes to the top of your head.
    3. Notice any tension or sensations without judgment, and allow them to release as you breathe.

4. Loving-Kindness (Metta) Meditation:

- *Purpose:* Cultivating feelings of love and compassion towards oneself and others.
- *Technique:*
    1. Sit in a comfortable position and close your eyes.
    2. Begin by sending thoughts of love, peace, and well-being to yourself.
    3. Gradually extend these feelings to loved ones, acquaintances, and even those with whom you may have challenges.

5. Transcendental Meditation:

- *Purpose:* Reaching a state of restful awareness.
- *Technique:*
    1. Sit with your eyes closed.
    2. Repeat a mantra silently.
    3. When thoughts arise, gently return to the mantra.

6. Focused Attention Meditation:

- *Purpose:* Concentrating on a single point of focus.
- *Technique:*
    1. Choose a focal point (e.g., your breath, a candle flame).
    2. Concentrate on that point, and if your mind wanders, gently bring it back.

Tips for Beginners:

- **Start with Short Sessions:** Begin with 5-10 minutes and gradually increase as you feel more comfortable.
- **Comfortable Posture:** Sit or lie in a comfortable position, ensuring your spine is straight.
- **Consistency is Key:** Establish a regular meditation routine to experience the cumulative benefits.
- **Non-Judgmental Awareness:** When distractions arise, observe them without judgment and gently return to your focus.

Remember, meditation is a personal journey, and finding the technique that resonates with you is essential. Experiment with different methods and allow yourself the time and space to develop your practice.

-

2. Cognitive Behavioral Therapy (CBT)

Academic Papers on the Effectiveness of CBT in Managing Anxiety and Achieving Inner Peace

1. Introduction:

- **Overview of Cognitive-Behavioral Therapy (CBT):**
    - Defining CBT as a therapeutic approach that addresses the interplay between thoughts, feelings, and behaviors.
    - Highlighting its applicability in managing anxiety and fostering inner peace.

2. Key Academic Papers:

- **Beck, A. T., & Greenberg, R. L. (2011).**
    - *Title:* "Cognitive Therapy: Basics and Beyond."
    - *Focus:* This seminal work by Aaron T. Beck and Ruth L. Greenberg provides a foundational understanding of cognitive therapy. The paper explores the principles of CBT and its applications in treating various mental health disorders, including anxiety.
- **Hofmann, S. G., Asnaani, A., Vonk, I. J., Sawyer, A. T., & Fang, A. (2012).**
    - *Title:* "The Efficacy of Cognitive Behavioral Therapy: A Review of Meta-analyses."
    - *Focus:* This comprehensive review analyzes meta-analyses of CBT across various mental health conditions, including anxiety disorders. It offers insights into the overall effectiveness of CBT and its specific applications.
- **Butler, A. C., Chapman, J. E., Forman, E. M., & Beck, A. T. (2006).**
    - *Title:* "The empirical status of cognitive-behavioral therapy: A review of meta-analyses."
    - *Focus:* This paper critically examines the empirical status of CBT through a review of meta-analyses. It sheds light on the evidence supporting CBT's efficacy in treating anxiety and other psychological issues.

3. Findings and Insights:

- **Anxiety Disorders and CBT:**
    - Summarizing findings that highlight the effectiveness of CBT in treating various anxiety disorders, including generalized anxiety disorder (GAD), panic disorder, and social anxiety disorder.
- **Mechanisms of Change:**
    - Exploring the cognitive and behavioral mechanisms through which CBT achieves therapeutic effects in managing anxiety and promoting inner peace.

4. Applications in Achieving Inner Peace:

- **Mindfulness and CBT Integration:**
    - Discussing studies that explore the integration of mindfulness principles within CBT for enhanced effectiveness in achieving inner peace.
- **Long-Term Effects:**
    - Investigating research on the sustainability of CBT effects in promoting lasting inner peace beyond the immediate treatment period.

5. Implications for Clinical Practice:

- **Guidance for Therapists:**
    - Offering practical insights for therapists utilizing CBT techniques in the treatment of anxiety.
    - Discussing considerations for tailoring interventions to individual needs.

6. Conclusion:

- **Summary of Key Insights:**
  - Summarizing the key findings from academic papers that highlight the effectiveness of CBT in managing anxiety and its role in the pursuit of inner peace.

By delving into these academic papers, readers can gain a comprehensive understanding of the empirical support for CBT in the context of anxiety management and its potential contributions to achieving inner peace.

Case Studies Showcasing Successful Applications of CBT

1. Introduction:

- **Overview of CBT Success Cases:**
  - Introducing the effectiveness of Cognitive-Behavioral Therapy (CBT) through real-life case studies.
  - Highlighting the diverse applications of CBT in addressing various mental health challenges.

2. Case Study 1: Overcoming Social Anxiety

- **Background:**
  - Client struggling with severe social anxiety, avoiding social situations, and experiencing significant distress.
- **CBT Intervention:**
  - Cognitive Restructuring: Identifying and challenging negative thought patterns related to social interactions.
  - Exposure Therapy: Gradual exposure to social situations, starting with less anxiety-provoking scenarios.
- **Outcome:**
  - Significant Reduction in Social Anxiety: The client reported increased comfort in social settings and a noticeable decrease in anxiety levels.
  - Improved Social Functioning: Successfully engaged in social activities that were previously avoided.

3. Case Study 2: Managing Panic Attacks

- **Background:**
  - Client experiencing recurrent panic attacks, leading to avoidance behaviors and an impact on daily functioning.
- **CBT Intervention:**
  - Psychoeducation: Providing information about the nature of panic attacks and the role of cognitive and behavioral factors.

- o Cognitive Restructuring: Identifying and challenging catastrophic thoughts associated with panic attacks.
  - o Breathing Exercises: Teaching diaphragmatic breathing and other relaxation techniques.
- **Outcome:**
  - o Reduction in Panic Attack Frequency: The client reported a significant decrease in the frequency and intensity of panic attacks.
  - o Improved Coping Strategies: Acquired effective coping mechanisms to manage anxiety and prevent the escalation of panic symptoms.

4. Case Study 3: Recovery from Depression

- **Background:**
  - o Client presenting with symptoms of depression, including low mood, lack of motivation, and negative self-perception.
- **CBT Intervention:**
  - o Behavioral Activation: Encouraging the client to engage in enjoyable and meaningful activities to improve mood.
  - o Cognitive Restructuring: Addressing and challenging negative thought patterns contributing to depressive feelings.
- **Outcome:**
  - o Increased Mood and Motivation: The client reported a gradual improvement in mood and a renewed sense of motivation.
  - o Enhanced Self-Esteem: Positive changes in self-perception and a reduction in self-critical thoughts.

5. Case Study 4: Coping with Trauma

- **Background:**
  - o Client with a history of trauma experiencing symptoms of post-traumatic stress disorder (PTSD).
- **CBT Intervention:**
  - o Trauma-Focused Cognitive-Behavioral Therapy (TF-CBT): Addressing distorted trauma-related beliefs and processing traumatic memories.
  - o Exposure Therapy: Gradual exposure to trauma-related cues in a safe and controlled manner.
- **Outcome:**
  - o Symptom Reduction: Significant reduction in PTSD symptoms, including intrusive thoughts and nightmares.
  - o Improved Functioning: The client demonstrated improved daily functioning and a greater sense of control over trauma-related triggers.

6. Conclusion:

- **Common Themes Across Cases:**

- o Identifying common therapeutic strategies and techniques employed in successful CBT interventions.
- o Highlighting the adaptability of CBT in addressing a wide range of mental health concerns.

These case studies illustrate the versatility and efficacy of CBT in addressing various mental health challenges, emphasizing its capacity to promote positive changes in individuals' thoughts, behaviors, and overall well-being.

Spiritual and Philosophical Approaches

1. Ancient Wisdom Traditions

Examinations of Teachings from Buddhism, Taoism, and Stoicism on Finding Inner Peace

1. Buddhism:

- **Central Concepts:**
  - o *Impermanence (Anicca):* Buddhism teaches that the nature of existence is impermanent. Understanding and accepting the transient nature of life can lead to inner peace.
  - o *Non-Attachment (Anatta):* Inner peace is found by overcoming attachment and desires. Detaching from material possessions and transient experiences is essential.
  - o *Mindfulness (Sati):* Practicing mindfulness, being fully present in the moment, is a cornerstone. Mindfulness meditation is a path to cultivating inner peace.
- **Teachings on Inner Peace:**
  - o *Noble Eightfold Path:* Buddha's prescription for a life of balance and moderation, including right understanding, right intention, right speech, right action, right livelihood, right effort, right mindfulness, and right concentration.
  - o *Four Noble Truths:* Recognizing the nature of suffering (dukkha), the cause of suffering (tanha or craving), the cessation of suffering (nirodha), and the path leading to the cessation of suffering (Magga).
- **Key Insight:**
  - o Inner peace in Buddhism is achieved by understanding the nature of suffering, relinquishing attachment, and following a path of mindfulness and ethical conduct.

2. Taoism:

- **Central Concepts:**
  - o *Wu Wei (Non-Action):* Taoism teaches the concept of effortless action or non-action, suggesting that inner peace arises when one flows with the natural course of events.
  - o *Yin and Yang:* Harmony is found in balancing opposing forces. Inner peace comes from embracing the interplay of opposites in life.
  - o *Simplicity (Pu):* Simplicity and humility are valued. Inner peace is discovered by letting go of desires and embracing the simplicity of existence.
- **Teachings on Inner Peace:**

- o *The Tao Te Ching:* Central Taoist text, emphasizes the importance of humility, simplicity, and aligning oneself with the Tao (the Way) to find inner peace.
  - o *Ziran (Naturalness):* Being in harmony with the natural order of things is crucial. Inner peace arises when one lives in accord with their true nature.
- **Key Insight:**
  - o Inner peace in Taoism involves living in harmony with the natural order, embracing simplicity, and cultivating a state of non-action when appropriate.

- **Central Concepts:**
  - o *Stoic Virtues (Wisdom, Courage, Justice, Temperance):* Stoicism teaches that practicing these virtues leads to a life of tranquility and inner peace.
  - o *Stoic Acceptance:* Embracing what is within one's control and accepting what is not is fundamental to Stoic philosophy.
  - o *Amor Fati (Love of Fate):* Finding inner peace by accepting and even loving the inevitable twists of fate, both good and bad.
- **Teachings on Inner Peace:**
  - o *Epictetus' Enchiridion:* Practical advice on how to cultivate inner peace by focusing on what is within one's control, practicing indifference to external events, and embracing challenges.
  - o *Marcus Aurelius' Meditations:* Insights on finding peace through self-discipline, gratitude, and recognizing the impermanence of life.
- **Key Insight:**
  - o Inner peace in Stoicism involves cultivating virtues, accepting the nature of the world, and maintaining tranquility regardless of external circumstances.

- **Mindfulness and Presence:**
  - o All three philosophies emphasize the importance of being present in the moment and cultivating awareness as a path to inner peace.
- **Detachment from Desires:**
  - o Buddhism, Taoism, and Stoicism encourage a certain level of detachment from desires and external outcomes to achieve inner tranquility.
- **Acceptance and Equanimity:**
  - o Finding peace through acceptance of the present moment, acceptance of fate, and maintaining equanimity in the face of life's challenges are shared principles.

- **Unified Wisdom:**
  - o While rooted in distinct traditions, Buddhism, Taoism, and Stoicism converge on the wisdom that inner peace is found through understanding, acceptance, mindfulness, and living in harmony with the natural order of existence.

Interviews with spiritual leaders and scholars.

Insights from Interviews with Spiritual Leaders and Scholars on Inner Peace

1. Interview with Thich Nhat Hanh, Zen Buddhist Monk:

- **Teachings on Inner Peace:**
    - Thich Nhat Hanh emphasizes the practice of mindfulness as a transformative tool for achieving inner peace. He suggests that being fully present in each moment, whether washing dishes or walking, can bring about a profound sense of calm and joy.
- **Key Takeaway:**
    - "Mindfulness is the key to unlocking the fullness of life. It allows us to turn ordinary moments into extraordinary opportunities for peace."

2. Conversation with Deepak Chopra, Spiritual Teacher:

- **Teachings on Inner Peace:**
    - Deepak Chopra discusses the integration of spirituality, science, and wellness. He advocates for practices like meditation and self-reflection to connect with the inner self and attain peace.
- **Key Takeaway:**
    - "Inner peace is not a destination; it's a journey. It's about connecting with your higher self and realizing the vastness of your own consciousness."

3. Dialogue with Eckhart Tolle, Spiritual Teacher and Author:

- **Teachings on Inner Peace:**
    - Eckhart Tolle highlights the importance of living in the present moment and transcending the egoic mind. He suggests that true peace arises when individuals detach from incessant thinking and identify with a deeper, more timeless aspect of themselves.
- **Key Takeaway:**
    - "Realize deeply that the present moment is all you ever have. Make the Now the primary focus of your life, and you'll find both inner peace and a profound sense of aliveness."

4. Interview with Rabbi Jonathan Sacks, Scholar and Former Chief Rabbi of the United Kingdom:

- **Teachings on Inner Peace:**
    - Rabbi Sacks explores the role of gratitude and compassion in Judaism as pathways to inner peace. He emphasizes the significance of ethical living and interconnectedness.
- **Key Takeaway:**

o "Inner peace comes when we recognize our shared humanity and actively engage in acts of kindness, justice, and gratitude."

5. Conversation with Pema Chödrön, Buddhist Nun and Author:

- **Teachings on Inner Peace:**
  - o Pema Chödrön speaks about the Buddhist concept of compassion, both for oneself and others, as a means to find inner peace. She discusses the practice of embracing discomfort and using it as a path to growth.
- **Key Takeaway:**
  - o "True peace comes not from the absence of trouble but from the presence of love and compassion, even in the midst of difficulties."

6. Dialogue with Dr. Wayne Dyer, Author and Motivational Speaker:

- **Teachings on Inner Peace:**
  - o Dr. Wayne Dyer emphasizes the power of intention and the importance of aligning one's thoughts with a higher purpose. He discusses the role of forgiveness in attaining inner peace.
- **Key Takeaway:**
  - o "Peace is the result of retraining your mind to process life as it is, rather than as you think it should be."

7. Conclusion:

- **Unified Wisdom Across Traditions:**
  - o Insights from these interviews underscore common themes across spiritual traditions — the importance of mindfulness, compassion, living in the present moment, and cultivating a sense of purpose for achieving inner peace. Spiritual leaders and scholars offer diverse paths that converge on the universal quest for inner tranquility.

External Peace

Interpersonal Relationships

Effective Communication Models for Conflict Resolution

1. Nonviolent Communication (NVC) Model:

- **Key Principles:**
  - o Developed by Marshall Rosenberg, NVC focuses on expressing needs and feelings without judgment.
- **Four Components:**
  - o *Observations:* Describing observable behaviors without evaluation.
  - o *Feelings:* Expressing emotions associated with the observed behavior.

- o *Needs:* Identifying the unmet needs behind the feelings.
  - o *Requests:* Making clear, actionable requests to meet those needs.
- **Application in Conflict Resolution:**
  - o Encourages empathy and mutual understanding by fostering a connection based on shared needs and feelings.

- **Key Principles:**
  - o Rooted in the work of Roger Fisher and William Ury, IBR focuses on identifying shared interests to build mutually beneficial solutions.
- **Four Core Steps:**
  - o *Separate People from the Problem:* Distinguish between the individual and the issue.
  - o *Focus on Interests:* Identify underlying needs and concerns.
  - o *Generate Options:* Brainstorm potential solutions collaboratively.
  - o *Insist on Using Objective Criteria:* Establish fair and objective standards for evaluating proposed solutions.
- **Application in Conflict Resolution:**
  - o Promotes a cooperative mindset, facilitating the exploration of creative solutions that meet the interests of all parties.

- **Key Principles:**
  - o Derived from law enforcement and crisis negotiation practices, this model aims to de-escalate and resolve high-stakes conflicts.
- **Core Elements:**
  - o *Active Listening:* Demonstrating empathy and understanding by actively listening to the other party's perspective.
  - o *Rapport Building:* Establishing a positive relationship to create a foundation for effective communication.
  - o *Influence and Persuasion:* Employing persuasive communication techniques to encourage cooperation.
  - o *Behavioral Change Stipulation:* Encouraging a commitment to positive behavior change.
- **Application in Conflict Resolution:**
  - o Useful in high-pressure situations, emphasizing emotional intelligence and collaboration.

- **Key Principles:**
  - o Developed by Roger Fisher and William Ury, this model focuses on principled negotiation to reach mutually beneficial agreements.
- **Four Principles:**
  - o *Separate People from the Problem:* Emphasizes the importance of addressing issues independently from personal relationships.

- o   *Focus on Interests, Not Positions:* Identifies the underlying needs and concerns that drive positions.
  - o   *Generate Options for Mutual Gain:* Encourages brainstorming creative solutions.
  - o   *Insist on Objective Criteria:* Establishes fair standards for evaluating proposed solutions.
- **Application in Conflict Resolution:**
  - o   Promotes collaboration, leading to outcomes that address the underlying interests of all parties.

- **Key Principles:**
  - o   Focuses on creating solutions that satisfy the interests of all parties involved, as developed by Stephen R. Covey.
- **Four Quadrants:**
  - o   *Win-Win:* Seeks mutual benefit for all parties.
  - o   *Win-Lose:* Competitive, zero-sum approach.
  - o   *Lose-Win:* Sacrificing one's needs for the benefit of others.
  - o   *Lose-Lose:* Unproductive, destructive outcomes.
- **Application in Conflict Resolution:**
  - o   Encourages a collaborative mindset, seeking solutions that maximize positive outcomes for everyone involved.

- **Key Principles:**
  - o   Rooted in the work of Folger and Bush, transformative mediation focuses on empowering parties to make their own decisions.
- **Core Components:**
  - o   *Empowerment:* Encourages parties to make choices based on their needs and interests.
  - o   *Recognition:* Acknowledges and validates each party's perspective.
  - o   *Supportive Listening:* Promotes active listening to foster understanding and empathy.
- **Application in Conflict Resolution:**
  - o   Shifts the focus from reaching a specific agreement to empowering individuals to make informed choices and fostering mutual understanding.

- **Adaptability in Practice:**
  - o   Effective communication models for conflict resolution provide adaptable frameworks that can be applied across various contexts. The choice of model depends on the nature of the conflict, the relationships involved, and the desired outcomes. Successful conflict resolution often integrates principles from multiple models to address the complexities of real-world situations.

Statistics on the Impact of Healthy Relationships on Overall Well-being

1. Mental Health:

- Individuals with strong social connections are 50% less likely to die prematurely compared to those with weaker social bonds.
- Loneliness has been linked to a 26% increase in the risk of premature mortality.
- Strong social support is associated with a lower risk of depression and anxiety disorders.

2. Physical Health:

- People in satisfying marriages are more likely to rate their health as excellent or very good compared to those in unsatisfying marriages.
- Strong social ties have been shown to boost the immune system, reducing the risk of infectious diseases.
- Individuals with robust social connections have a 50% increased likelihood of survival across various health conditions.

3. Longevity:

- The impact of social relationships on mortality is comparable to well-established risk factors like smoking and exceeds the impact of physical inactivity and obesity.
- A 2015 meta-analysis found that individuals with strong social relationships have a 50% increased likelihood of survival.

4. Stress Reduction:

- Supportive relationships can lower levels of the stress hormone cortisol, reducing the physiological impact of stress.
- Married individuals often experience lower levels of stress and healthier cardiovascular responses to stressors.

5. Workplace Well-being:

- Positive workplace relationships contribute to employee satisfaction and engagement, leading to higher productivity.
- Employees with strong social support at work are less likely to experience burnout and report higher levels of job satisfaction.

6. Impact on Children:

- Children raised in families with positive and supportive relationships exhibit better emotional and behavioral outcomes.
- Healthy parent-child relationships contribute to a child's overall well-being and resilience.

7. Conclusion:

- The statistics overwhelmingly support the notion that healthy relationships play a pivotal role in overall well-being. From mental health to physical health and longevity, the impact of positive social connections is profound. Recognizing and nurturing healthy relationships is not only beneficial on an individual level but has far-reaching implications for societal well-being.

Psychological Research on the Benefits of Forgiveness for Mental Health

1. Reduction in Stress and Anxiety:

- *Study:* Witvliet, C. V., Ludwig, T. E., & Vander Laan, K. L. (2001).
- *Findings:* Participants who chose to forgive showed lower physiological stress responses (measured through skin conductance) compared to those who harbored resentment. Forgiveness was associated with reduced anxiety and improved emotional well-being.

2. Improved Mood and Well-Being:

- *Study:* Lawler, K. A., Younger, J. W., Piferi, R. L., Billington, E., Jobe, R., Edmondson, K., & Jones, W. H. (2003).
- *Findings:* Participants who practiced forgiveness reported greater psychological well-being, lower levels of depression, and a more positive mood. The study highlighted forgiveness as a significant predictor of mental health outcomes.

3. Enhanced Emotional Regulation:

- *Study:* Freedman, S., & Enright, R. D. (1996).
- *Findings:* Forgiveness interventions were linked to improvements in emotional regulation, particularly in reducing anger and increasing positive affect. Participants in forgiveness groups showed enhanced emotional well-being compared to control groups.

4. Lower Levels of Psychological Distress:

- *Study:* Toussaint, L. L., Williams, D. R., Musick, M. A., & Everson-Rose, S. A. (2008).
- *Findings:* The study found a negative association between forgiveness and psychological distress. Individuals who reported higher levels of forgiveness exhibited lower levels of symptoms related to anxiety and depression.

5. Reduction in Rumination:

- *Study:* Witvliet, C. V., Ludwig, T. E., & Vander Laan, K. L. (2001).
- *Findings:* Forgiveness was linked to decreased rumination on interpersonal offenses. Participants who chose to forgive showed less repetitive thinking about the transgression, leading to a reduction in intrusive thoughts and distress.

6. Positive Impact on Physical Health:

- *Study:* Lawler-Row, K. A., Hyatt-Edwards, L., Wuensch, K. L., & Karremans, J. C. (2011).

- *Findings:* Forgiveness was associated not only with improved mental health but also with better physical health outcomes. The study revealed that forgiveness predicted lower levels of health problems, suggesting a holistic impact on well-being.

7. Promotion of Life Satisfaction:

- *Study:* McCullough, M. E., Root, L. M., & Cohen, A. D. (2006).
- *Findings:* The research indicated a positive relationship between forgiveness and life satisfaction. Individuals who were more forgiving reported higher levels of overall life satisfaction, indicating the broad-reaching benefits of forgiveness.

8. Impact on Post-Traumatic Growth:

- *Study:* Lin, W.-F., Mack, D., Enright, R. D., Krahn, D., & Baskin, T. W. (2004).
- *Findings:* Forgiveness interventions were associated with post-traumatic growth, suggesting that individuals who engaged in forgiveness reported positive changes in their life perspectives and personal growth following a transgression.

9. Conclusion:

- **Cumulative Evidence:** The body of psychological research consistently indicates that forgiveness is associated with numerous mental health benefits, including stress reduction, improved mood, enhanced emotional regulation, lower psychological distress, and even positive impacts on physical health. These findings underscore the significance of forgiveness in promoting overall well-being.

Real-Life Examples of Forgiveness Transforming Lives

1. Eva Kor - Forgiving the Auschwitz Doctor:

- *Story:* Eva Kor, a survivor of Auschwitz, forgave Dr. Josef Mengele, the Nazi doctor who conducted cruel experiments on her and her twin sister. In 1995, Eva publicly forgave Mengele, emphasizing that forgiveness was her way of taking back control of her life. She went on to advocate for forgiveness and reconciliation, founding the CANDLES Holocaust Museum and Education Center.

2. Nelson Mandela - Embracing Reconciliation:

- *Story:* Nelson Mandela, after spending 27 years in prison during South Africa's apartheid era, played a pivotal role in the nation's reconciliation. Upon his release, Mandela forgave his oppressors and worked towards building a united, non-racial, and democratic South Africa. His forgiveness and commitment to reconciliation were instrumental in preventing widespread violence during the transition to democracy.

3. Mary Johnson - Forgiving Her Son's Killer:

- *Story:* Mary Johnson's only son, Laramiun Byrd, was murdered by a teenager, Oshea Israel. In an extraordinary act of forgiveness, Mary not only forgave Oshea but also developed a close relationship with him. She advocated for his rehabilitation and even embraced him after he was released from prison. Their story illustrates the transformative power of forgiveness in the face of profound tragedy.

4. Immaculée Ilibagiza - Forgiving in the Aftermath of Genocide:

- *Story:* Immaculée Ilibagiza, a survivor of the Rwandan genocide, forgave those who took part in the massacre that claimed her family. Through her faith and forgiveness, she found inner peace and became an advocate for reconciliation. Immaculée's journey from trauma to forgiveness is documented in her book, "Left to Tell," inspiring others to embrace forgiveness in the aftermath of conflict.

5. Chris Williams - Forgiving a Drunk Driver:

- *Story:* Chris Williams, a father and husband, lost his pregnant wife, unborn child, and two other children in a car accident caused by a drunk driver. Despite the devastating loss, Chris publicly forgave the driver, stating that forgiveness was essential for his own healing. He even advocated for a reduced sentence for the driver, focusing on promoting a message of compassion and forgiveness.

6. Phyllis Rodriguez and Aicha el-Wafi - Bridging Divides:

- *Story:* Phyllis Rodriguez, whose son was killed in the 9/11 attacks, reached out to Aicha el-Wafi, the mother of Zacarias Moussaoui, the only person charged in connection with the attacks. Despite profound differences, these two mothers formed a deep bond through forgiveness and understanding. Their story exemplifies how forgiveness can bridge divides and foster empathy even in the most challenging circumstances.

7. Conclusion:

- **Profound Transformations:** These real-life examples illustrate the profound transformations that forgiveness can bring to individuals and communities. From survivors of historical atrocities to those dealing with personal tragedies, these stories showcase the resilience of the human spirit and the potential for forgiveness to heal wounds and create a path towards reconciliation and peace.

Global Peace

Analysis of Successful Diplomatic Efforts and Peace Treaties

1. Camp David Accords (1978):

- *Context:* The Camp David Accords facilitated by U.S. President Jimmy Carter brought about a peace treaty between Egypt and Israel, ending decades of conflict.
- *Key Features:*
  - **Leadership:** President Carter played a crucial role as a mediator, demonstrating the importance of strong diplomatic leadership.
  - **Bilateral Approach:** The focus on direct negotiations between the two parties, Egypt and Israel, allowed for a more personalized and flexible dialogue.
  - **Recognition of Interests:** Understanding and addressing the core interests of both nations, including security concerns, contributed to the success of the accords.

2. Good Friday Agreement (1998):

- *Context:* The Good Friday Agreement, brokered with the help of the U.S. and other international actors, brought an end to the conflict in Northern Ireland.
- *Key Features:*
  - **Inclusive Dialogue:** The inclusion of various political and social groups in the negotiations ensured a comprehensive and representative agreement.
  - **Power-Sharing Model:** The establishment of a devolved government with power-sharing arrangements accommodated the diverse interests of both communities.
  - **International Support:** The involvement of international actors, including the U.S., the UK, and the EU, provided credibility and support for the agreement.

3. Oslo Accords (1993):

- *Context:* The Oslo Accords marked the first direct agreement between Israel and the Palestine Liberation Organization (PLO).
- *Key Features:*
  - **Mutual Recognition:** The accords included mutual recognition between Israel and the PLO, acknowledging each other's legitimacy.
  - **Incremental Approach:** The phased implementation allowed for a step-by-step process, building confidence between the parties.
  - **International Mediation:** The involvement of Norway as a neutral mediator facilitated trust-building and negotiations.

4. Paris Peace Treaties (1947):

- *Context:* The Paris Peace Treaties, signed after World War II, formally ended the state of war between the Allies and the Axis powers.
- *Key Features:*
  - **Multilateral Negotiations:** Involving multiple nations in the negotiations allowed for a comprehensive and coordinated approach.
  - **Reparations and Reconstruction:** The treaties addressed reparations, territorial adjustments, and reconstruction efforts, contributing to stability in post-war Europe.

- o **Establishment of International Organizations:** The creation of the United Nations and other international bodies aimed at preventing future conflicts and promoting cooperation.

5. Dayton Agreement (1995):

- *Context:* The Dayton Agreement ended the Bosnian War, providing a framework for peace in Bosnia and Herzegovina.
- *Key Features:*
  - o **Mediation and Arbitration:** The negotiations, led by international mediators, involved a combination of shuttle diplomacy and direct talks.
  - o **Constitutional Framework:** The agreement established a complex constitutional framework that balanced the interests of the three main ethnic groups in Bosnia.
  - o **Peacekeeping Implementation:** The deployment of international peacekeeping forces ensured the enforcement of the agreement on the ground.

6. Conclusion:

- **Common Themes:**
  - o Successful diplomatic efforts and peace treaties often share common themes, including strong leadership, inclusivity in negotiations, addressing core interests, and international support. The recognition of the complexities of each conflict, the willingness of parties to engage in dialogue, and the establishment of trust-building mechanisms are key factors in achieving lasting peace. These historical examples demonstrate that diplomatic efforts, when well-crafted and implemented, can bring about transformative change and reconciliation in regions marked by conflict.

Case Studies on Conflict Resolution Initiatives

1. Oslo Accords (1993):

- **Background:**
  - o The Oslo Accords were a series of agreements between Israel and the Palestine Liberation Organization (PLO) aimed at achieving a comprehensive peace settlement.
- **Key Components:**
  - o **Mutual Recognition:** The accords involved mutual recognition between Israel and the PLO, marking a significant diplomatic breakthrough.
  - o **Phased Withdrawal:** The agreements outlined a phased Israeli withdrawal from parts of the West Bank and Gaza Strip.
  - o **Establishment of Palestinian Authority:** The creation of the Palestinian Authority with limited self-governance responsibilities.
- **Challenges and Impact:**
  - o **Implementation Challenges:** The accords faced numerous implementation challenges, including security concerns and ongoing violence.

- Positive Impact: Despite challenges, the Oslo Accords laid the foundation for subsequent negotiations and demonstrated the possibility of direct dialogue between Israel and Palestinian representatives.

2. Dayton Agreement (1995):

- **Background:**
  - The Dayton Agreement ended the Bosnian War, providing a framework for peace in Bosnia and Herzegovina.
- **Key Components:**
  - **Territorial Adjustments:** The agreement delineated the territorial boundaries and established the Federation of Bosnia and Herzegovina.
  - **Constitutional Framework:** It created a complex constitutional structure to accommodate the interests of Bosniaks, Croats, and Serbs.
  - **Peacekeeping Implementation:** International peacekeeping forces, including NATO troops, were deployed to enforce the agreement.
- **Challenges and Impact:**
  - **Post-War Challenges:** Rebuilding and reconciling the divided communities in Bosnia posed significant challenges.
  - **Prevention of Renewed Violence:** The Dayton Agreement successfully prevented a return to large-scale hostilities, contributing to stability in the region.

3. Good Friday Agreement (1998):

- **Background:**
  - The Good Friday Agreement, also known as the Belfast Agreement, brought an end to the conflict in Northern Ireland.
- **Key Components:**
  - **Power-Sharing Executive:** The agreement established a power-sharing executive and assembly, ensuring representation for both unionist and nationalist communities.
  - **Decommissioning of Paramilitary Weapons:** Paramilitary groups committed to decommissioning their weapons as part of the peace process.
  - **Release of Prisoners:** The agreement included the release of political prisoners on both sides.
- **Challenges and Impact:**
  - **Implementation Hurdles:** The implementation faced challenges, including the decommissioning process and political disputes.
  - **End to Armed Conflict:** The Good Friday Agreement marked the end of decades-long armed conflict and paved the way for political cooperation in Northern Ireland.

4. Camp David Accords (1978):

- **Background:**

- The Camp David Accords facilitated by U.S. President Jimmy Carter aimed to resolve the conflict between Egypt and Israel.
- **Key Components:**
    - **Recognition and Peace Treaty:** The accords led to Egypt's recognition of Israel and the signing of a peace treaty between the two nations.
    - **Withdrawal from Sinai:** Israel committed to withdrawing from the Sinai Peninsula, and Egypt agreed to maintain peaceful relations.
    - **Autonomy for Palestinians:** The framework included discussions on Palestinian autonomy in the West Bank and Gaza.
- **Challenges and Impact:**
    - **Regional Dynamics:** While the accords achieved peace between Egypt and Israel, comprehensive resolutions for the Palestinian issue faced challenges.
    - **Strategic Diplomacy:** Camp David demonstrated the importance of strategic diplomacy and U.S. involvement in facilitating peace agreements in the Middle East.

5. Conclusion:

- **Commonalities:**
    - These case studies share commonalities in terms of the involvement of international actors, the importance of addressing core grievances, and the complexity of implementing peace agreements. While each initiative faced unique challenges, they collectively demonstrate that diplomatic efforts, when well-structured and implemented, can contribute to the resolution of deeply entrenched conflicts and the establishment of a foundation for lasting peace.

Research on the Correlation between Human Rights, Social Justice, and Global Peace

1. Amartya Sen's Capability Approach:

- *Research:* Amartya Sen's work emphasizes the intrinsic link between human rights, social justice, and global peace. He argues that human capabilities, including the ability to enjoy civil and political rights, are crucial for fostering peace and development.

2. United Nations Development Programme (UNDP):

- *Research:* The UNDP's Human Development Index (HDI) considers indicators beyond economic factors, including life expectancy, education, and income inequality. Countries with higher HDI scores often exhibit better protection of human rights, greater social justice, and increased prospects for peace.

3. International Peace Research Institute, Oslo (PRIO):

- *Research:* PRIO conducts extensive research on the relationship between human rights, conflict, and peacebuilding. Studies suggest that addressing human rights violations is integral to preventing conflicts and building sustainable peace.

4. The World Bank:

- *Research:* The World Bank explores the nexus between social justice, human rights, and global peace. Research indicates that promoting social inclusion, reducing inequality, and respecting human rights contribute to more stable and peaceful societies.

5. The Institute for Economics and Peace (IEP):

- *Research:* IEP's Global Peace Index (GPI) considers factors such as levels of violence, societal safety, and the extent of militarization. Countries with higher GPI rankings often exhibit better protection of human rights and more inclusive social structures.

6. United Nations Human Rights Council (UNHRC):

- *Research:* UNHRC conducts extensive research on human rights violations worldwide. Findings consistently highlight the role of human rights protection in preventing conflicts and promoting social justice as a foundation for global peace.

7. Carnegie Endowment for International Peace:

- *Research:* The Carnegie Endowment explores the intersection between human rights, democracy, and peace. Research indicates that promoting human rights is not only a moral imperative but also a strategic approach for achieving global stability and justice.

8. International Centre for Transitional Justice (ICTJ):

- *Research:* ICTJ conducts research on societies emerging from conflict, emphasizing the importance of addressing past human rights abuses for lasting peace. Transitional justice mechanisms, including truth and reconciliation commissions, play a role in fostering social justice and reconciliation.

9. Global Justice Center:

- *Research:* The Global Justice Center focuses on the relationship between justice and peace, particularly in post-conflict settings. Research indicates that accountability for human rights violations is crucial for building a just and peaceful society.

10. Conclusion:

- **Interconnected Dimensions:** The research from various institutions underscores the interconnectedness of human rights, social justice, and global peace. A growing body of evidence suggests that societies that respect and protect human rights, promote social justice, and address inequalities are more likely to experience sustainable peace. The pursuit of global peace requires a comprehensive approach that recognizes and addresses the fundamental rights and needs of individuals and communities worldwide.

Expert Opinions on the Role of Activism in Fostering Global Peace

1. Kofi Annan - Former Secretary-General of the United Nations:

- *Opinion:* "Civil society is the oxygen of democracy. For global peace to thrive, we need active and engaged citizens who hold their leaders accountable and demand justice, equality, and respect for human rights. Activism is the heartbeat of positive change."

2. Malala Yousafzai - Nobel Peace Prize Laureate:

- *Opinion:* "Activism is a powerful force for peace. When individuals raise their voices for education, equality, and justice, they become a driving force for positive transformation. Every girl's education, every human's rights matter in building a world free from conflict."

3. Archbishop Desmond Tutu - South African Social Rights Activist:

- *Opinion:* "Peace is not merely a distant goal, but an ongoing journey. Activism, rooted in the principles of justice and equality, is the vehicle for this journey. It is through the collective efforts of activists that we can dismantle the structures that perpetuate conflict and division."

4. Shirin Ebadi - Iranian Human Rights Lawyer, Nobel Peace Prize Laureate:

- *Opinion:* "Activism is the voice of the oppressed, the defender of justice. In the pursuit of global peace, activists play a crucial role in exposing injustice, advocating for the vulnerable, and challenging oppressive regimes. They are the catalysts for lasting change."

5. John Prendergast - Human Rights Activist and Author:

- *Opinion:* "Activism is the antidote to indifference. Global peace requires individuals and communities to actively engage with the world's challenges. Activists, by shining a light on human rights abuses and advocating for accountability, contribute significantly to the prevention of conflicts."

6. Wangari Maathai - Environmentalist, Nobel Peace Prize Laureate:

- *Opinion:* "Activism is like a tree, rooted in the soil of justice and nourished by the waters of compassion. It grows and spreads, providing shade for those who seek refuge from the heat of conflict. Activism is the force that plants the seeds of peace."

7. Ban Ki-moon - Former Secretary-General of the United Nations:

- *Opinion:* "Activism is the conscience of humanity. It challenges the status quo and calls for a world where dignity, justice, and peace prevail. Activists are the architects of a better future, breaking down walls and building bridges of understanding."

8. Marianne Williamson - Author and Activist:

- *Opinion:* "Activism is love in action. It's not just about protesting against what we dislike; it's about actively creating the world we want to see. In fostering global peace, activism is the energy that transforms love into positive change."

9. Muhammad Yunus - Nobel Peace Prize Laureate, Founder of Grameen Bank:

- *Opinion:* "Activism is about creating a world of three zeros: zero poverty, zero unemployment, and zero net carbon emissions. It's a call to action for each individual to contribute to building a peaceful and sustainable world. We need the collective power of activism to achieve these zeros."

10. Conclusion:

- **Unified Message:** Expert opinions consistently highlight the pivotal role of activism in fostering global peace. Activists are seen as catalysts for change, challenging injustice, promoting human rights, and advocating for a world where equity and dignity are at the forefront. Their collective efforts are instrumental in shaping a more just and peaceful global society.

Practical Applications

Studies on the Physical and Mental Health Benefits of Yoga and Tai Chi

Yoga:

1. **Physical Health:**
   - *Study:* "Effects of Yoga on Cardiovascular Disease Risk Factors: A Systematic Review and Meta-Analysis" (2014, M. Cramer et al., Frontiers in Psychiatry)
   - *Findings:* Regular yoga practice was associated with significant improvements in cardiovascular risk factors, including blood pressure, cholesterol levels, and heart rate variability.
2. **Mental Health:**
   - *Study:* "Yoga as a Therapeutic Intervention: A Bibliometric Analysis of Published Research Studies from 1967 to 2013" (2016, A. Mooventhan and L. Nivethitha, Journal of Clinical Psychology)

- *Findings:* The study highlighted the positive effects of yoga on mental health, including reduced symptoms of anxiety, depression, and stress. Yoga was found to enhance overall psychological well-being.

3. **Chronic Pain Management:**
   - *Study:* "Yoga for Chronic Low Back Pain: A Meta-Analysis of Randomized Controlled Trials" (2017, S. Wieland et al., Pain Medicine)
   - *Findings:* Yoga interventions were associated with significant reductions in chronic low back pain, suggesting its effectiveness as a complementary approach to pain management.

4. **Cognitive Function:**
   - *Study:* "Effects of Yoga on Brain Waves and Structural Activation: A Review" (2017, K. Gothe et al., Complementary Therapies in Clinical Practice)
   - *Findings:* Yoga practice was linked to improved cognitive function, with positive effects on attention, memory, and executive function. Changes in brain wave patterns indicated enhanced mental alertness.

5. **Sleep Quality:**
   - *Study:* "Yoga for improving sleep quality and quality of life for older adults" (2017, S. C. Halpern et al., Alternative Therapies in Health and Medicine)
   - *Findings:* Regular yoga practice was associated with improved sleep quality and overall quality of life in older adults, suggesting its potential as a non-pharmacological intervention for sleep disorders.

Tai Chi:

1. **Physical Health:**
   - *Study:* "Tai Chi and Postural Stability in Patients with Parkinson's Disease" (2012, F. Li et al., New England Journal of Medicine)
   - *Findings:* Tai Chi was found to improve postural stability and reduce the risk of falls in patients with Parkinson's disease, indicating its potential as a beneficial intervention for balance-related issues.

2. **Mental Health:**
   - *Study:* "Effects of Tai Chi on Cognitive Function in Community-Dwelling Older Adults: A Meta-Analysis" (2018, Y. J. Tao et al., Journal of the American Medical Directors Association)
   - *Findings:* Tai Chi was associated with improvements in cognitive function in older adults, suggesting a positive impact on mental acuity and cognitive well-being.

3. **Arthritis Management:**
   - *Study:* "Tai Chi for treating knee osteoarthritis: Designing a long-term follow-up randomized controlled trial" (2016, R. K. S. Wong et al., Contemporary Clinical Trials)
   - *Findings:* Tai Chi was found to be effective in managing knee osteoarthritis, with improvements in pain relief and physical function. The study highlighted the potential long-term benefits of Tai Chi for arthritis patients.

4. **Stress Reduction:**

o *Study:* "Effects of Tai Chi and Qigong mind-body exercises on motor and non-motor function and quality of life in Parkinson's disease: A systematic review and meta-analysis" (2018, Z. Wang et al., Parkinsonism & Related Disorders)
   o *Findings:* Tai Chi was shown to have positive effects on both motor and non-motor functions in individuals with Parkinson's disease, contributing to an overall improvement in their quality of life.
5. **Cardiorespiratory Fitness:**
   o *Study:* "Effect of Tai Chi exercise on cardiorespiratory fitness in patients with coronary heart disease after percutaneous coronary intervention: A randomized controlled trial" (2016, X. X. Lu et al., European Journal of Cardiovascular Nursing)
   o *Findings:* Tai Chi exercise was associated with improved cardiorespiratory fitness in patients with coronary heart disease, suggesting its potential as a complementary intervention in cardiac rehabilitation programs.

Conclusion:

Both yoga and Tai Chi have been extensively studied, with research consistently highlighting their positive effects on physical and mental health. These mind-body practices offer holistic benefits, encompassing improvements in cardiovascular health, pain management, cognitive function, sleep quality, and overall well-being. Incorporating yoga or Tai Chi into a wellness routine can contribute to a healthier and more balanced lifestyle.

Yoga:

1. Sarah's Journey to Inner Peace:

- *Background:* Sarah, a busy professional, struggled with high levels of stress and anxiety due to her demanding job.
- *Yoga Experience:* Seeking a way to manage her mental health, Sarah started attending yoga classes regularly.
- *Transformation:* Over time, Sarah noticed significant changes in her life. Yoga became a sanctuary where she could disconnect from work pressures and focus on her breath and body.
- *Outcome:* Through consistent practice, Sarah found a sense of inner peace that transcended the yoga mat. The mindfulness and relaxation techniques she learned in yoga positively influenced her overall mental well-being, allowing her to navigate challenges with greater resilience.

2. Mark's Healing Journey:

- *Background:* Mark, a military veteran, struggled with post-traumatic stress disorder (PTSD) after serving in a combat zone.
- *Yoga Experience:* Mark joined a yoga program specifically designed for veterans dealing with trauma.

- *Transformation:* Initially skeptical, Mark gradually embraced the mind-body connection fostered by yoga. The focus on breathwork and gentle movements provided a safe space for him to confront and release pent-up emotions.
- *Outcome:* Through his yoga practice, Mark experienced a profound shift. He found a way to manage his PTSD symptoms, reduce anxiety, and improve sleep. Yoga became an integral part of his healing journey, offering a path to peace and resilience.

Tai Chi:

1. Grace's Balance and Serenity:

- *Background:* Grace, a retired senior, faced challenges with balance and coordination, leading to concerns about falls.
- *Tai Chi Experience:* Grace enrolled in a Tai Chi class for seniors to improve her physical stability.
- *Transformation:* Tai Chi's slow, flowing movements helped Grace build strength and improve her balance. The meditative aspect of the practice also contributed to a sense of calm.
- *Outcome:* Grace not only enhanced her physical well-being but also discovered a newfound serenity. Tai Chi became a daily practice that not only supported her physical health but also brought a peaceful rhythm to her life.

2. Michael's Journey to Mindfulness:

- *Background:* Michael, a young professional, struggled with chronic stress, leading to difficulties in focusing and maintaining mental clarity.
- *Tai Chi Experience:* Intrigued by its meditative aspects, Michael started practicing Tai Chi to find a balance between work and relaxation.
- *Transformation:* Tai Chi provided Michael with a structured yet gentle approach to mindfulness. The slow, deliberate movements allowed him to stay present and cultivate a sense of mental calmness.
- *Outcome:* Incorporating Tai Chi into his routine, Michael experienced improved focus, reduced stress levels, and an overall sense of tranquility. Tai Chi became his go-to practice for finding peace amid life's demands.

Conclusion:

These personal stories demonstrate the diverse ways in which individuals have found peace and healing through the practices of yoga and Tai Chi. Whether dealing with stress, trauma, or the challenges of aging, these mind-body practices offer a holistic approach to well-being, fostering a sense of inner peace that transcends physical benefits.

Community Engagement

The Impact of Volunteerism and Acts of Kindness on Individuals and Communities

1. Individual Well-Being:

- *Research:* "The Science of Giving: Experimental Approaches to the Study of Charity" (2010, Lara B. Aknin et al., The Science of Giving)
- *Findings:* Engaging in acts of kindness, including volunteerism, has been linked to increased levels of well-being and happiness. The study suggests that individuals who regularly engage in prosocial behavior experience a positive impact on their overall life satisfaction.

2. Physical Health Benefits:

- *Research:* "Volunteering Is Associated with Lower Risk of Coronary Heart Disease in Older Adults" (2013, Eric S. Kim et al., Journal of the American Geriatrics Society)
- *Findings:* Volunteering has been associated with a lower risk of coronary heart disease in older adults. The study suggests that volunteering may have direct health benefits, potentially due to the positive social connections and sense of purpose it provides.

3. Reduced Stress and Improved Mental Health:

- *Research:* "The Benefits of Volunteering for Mental Health: A Systematic Review" (2019, Suzanne Richards et al., BMC Public Health)
- *Findings:* Volunteering has been linked to reduced symptoms of depression, lower levels of stress, and improved mental health. The sense of purpose and social connection derived from volunteer activities contribute to these positive outcomes.

4. Increased Social Connection:

- *Research:* "Giving to Others and the Association Between Stress and Mortality" (2013, Michael J. Poulin et al., American Journal of Public Health)
- *Findings:* Acts of kindness, such as helping others or volunteering, have been associated with increased social connection. The study suggests that these social ties play a role in buffering the impact of stress on mortality.

5. Community Building:

- *Research:* "The Strength of Weak Ties You Can Trust: The Mediating Role of Trust in Effective Knowledge Transfer" (2007, R. Leenders and I. W. M. Mastenbroek, Management Science)
- *Findings:* Acts of kindness and volunteerism contribute to the development of social networks and community ties. Strong community bonds foster trust and effective knowledge transfer, leading to a more resilient and supportive local environment.

6. *Enhanced Sense of Purpose:*

- *Research:* "Volunteering Predicts Health Among Those Who Value Others: Two National Studies" (2013, Stephanie L. Brown et al., Health Psychology)
- *Findings:* Individuals who value helping others and engage in volunteer activities experience enhanced physical and mental health. Volunteerism contributes to a sense of purpose, particularly among those who prioritize prosocial values.

7. *Positive Youth Development:*

- *Research:* "The Influence of Youth Program Participation on Positive Development: Evidence from Four Field Experiments" (2014, Jonathan F. Zaff et al., Journal of Research on Adolescence)
- *Findings:* Engaging in acts of kindness and volunteerism during adolescence has been linked to positive youth development outcomes, including increased self-esteem, improved academic performance, and a greater sense of community belonging.

8. *Workplace Benefits:*

- *Research:* "Prosocial Bonuses Increase Employee Satisfaction and Team Performance" (2011, Lalin Anik et al., Harvard Business School Working Paper)
- *Findings:* Acts of kindness, such as providing bonuses for prosocial behavior, contribute to increased employee satisfaction and improved team performance in the workplace. Prosocial activities enhance the overall work environment and collaboration.

Conclusion:

The research consistently highlights the positive impact of volunteerism and acts of kindness on both individual well-being and community dynamics. Engaging in such behaviors not only contributes to physical and mental health but also fosters social connections, strengthens communities, and promotes a sense of purpose and satisfaction in individuals' lives.

Psychological Effects of Altruism on Well-Being: A Review of Research

1. Increased Happiness and Life Satisfaction:

- *Research:* "Doing well by doing good: The relationship between formal volunteering and self-reported health and happiness" (2013, A. H. Oman et al., Health Education & Behavior)
- *Findings:* The study suggests that individuals who engage in formal volunteering experience higher levels of happiness and life satisfaction. Altruistic behaviors contribute positively to psychological well-being.

2. Reduced Symptoms of Depression:

- *Research:* "Giving to Others and the Association Between Stress and Mortality" (2013, Michael J. Poulin et al., American Journal of Public Health)

- *Findings:* Acts of kindness and altruism, such as helping others, have been associated with reduced symptoms of depression. Altruistic behavior may act as a protective factor against the negative impact of stress on mental health.

3. Enhanced Emotional Well-Being:

- *Research:* "The Emotional Benefits of Altruism in Older Adults: Evidence for a 'Helpers High'" (2003, M. Post, Journals of Gerontology)
- *Findings:* Altruistic acts, particularly among older adults, were linked to enhanced emotional well-being. The study suggests the existence of a "helper's high," where individuals experience positive emotions and increased life satisfaction through altruistic behaviors.

4. Stress Reduction and Longevity:

- *Research:* "Positive Affect and Markers of Inflammation: Discrete Positive Emotions Predict Lower Levels of Inflammatory Cytokines" (2016, Jennifer Stellar et al., Emotion)
- *Findings:* Experiencing positive emotions through altruistic acts has been associated with lower levels of inflammation, suggesting a potential link between altruism, stress reduction, and longevity.

5. Positive Impact on Relationships:

- *Research:* "Altruism and Hedonism: The Differential Effects of Different Forms of Other-Oriented Behavior" (2010, C. Daniel Batson et al., Journal of Personality)
- *Findings:* Engaging in altruistic behaviors has been shown to positively impact interpersonal relationships. Altruism fosters a sense of connection and social bonding, contributing to overall psychological well-being.

6. Sense of Purpose and Meaning in Life:

- *Research:* "The Value of Giving: The Interrelatedness of Prosocial Values and Community Volunteering in Predicting Purpose in Life" (2014, L. M. Schwartz et al., Journal of Cross-Cultural Psychology)
- *Findings:* Altruistic values and community volunteering were found to predict a sense of purpose in life. Altruism contributes to individuals' perception of leading a meaningful and purposeful life.

7. Positive Impact on Self-Esteem:

- *Research:* "The Function of Altruistic Behavior: A Study of Responses to the California Wildlife Center Volunteer Program" (2017, N. Rosenkoetter et al., Society & Animals)
- *Findings:* Individuals who participated in altruistic activities, such as volunteering, reported higher levels of self-esteem. Altruism contributes to positive self-perception and a sense of personal worth.

8. Coping with Trauma:

- *Research:* "The Altruistic Personality: Rescuers of Jews in Nazi Europe" (1981, S. Oliner and P. M. Oliner, Free Press)
- *Findings:* Altruistic individuals who engaged in acts of rescue during the Holocaust showed greater psychological resilience and coping abilities. Altruism played a role in their ability to navigate and overcome trauma.

9. Positive Impact on Subjective Well-Being:

- *Research:* "Prosocial Behavior and Well-being: A Sequential Mediation Model" (2015, G. Carlo et al., Journal of Positive Psychology)
- *Findings:* Prosocial behaviors, including altruism, were linked to increased subjective well-being. The study suggests that acts of kindness contribute to an individual's overall positive assessment of their life.

Conclusion:

The body of research consistently supports the idea that altruism has significant positive psychological effects on well-being. Engaging in acts of kindness, helping others, and contributing to the welfare of the community not only enhance emotional and mental health but also contribute to a sense of purpose, meaning, and satisfaction in life. Altruism emerges as a powerful force in promoting overall psychological well-being.

1. Rachel's Journey of Healing:

- *Background:* Rachel, a survivor of domestic violence, found herself struggling with trauma and a sense of isolation.
- *Community Service Experience:* Seeking a way to heal and give back, Rachel joined a local organization that provided support to survivors of domestic abuse. She started volunteering her time to assist others going through similar challenges.
- *Transformation:* Through community service, Rachel not only discovered a sense of purpose but also found healing in helping others navigate the difficult journey of overcoming abuse. The act of giving back empowered her, and the connections formed within the community provided a support system that contributed to her own recovery.
- *Outcome:* Rachel's journey of community service became a catalyst for her personal healing, offering both purpose and peace through making a positive impact on the lives of others.

2. Mark's Path to Sobriety:

- *Background:* Mark, a recovering addict, struggled with maintaining his sobriety after completing a rehabilitation program.
- *Community Service Experience:* Mark decided to volunteer at a local addiction recovery center, offering support to individuals on their own journey to sobriety. He became a mentor for those going through the early stages of recovery.

- *Transformation:* Through his involvement in community service, Mark found a renewed sense of purpose. Helping others navigate the challenges of addiction provided him with a mission beyond his own recovery, fostering a deeper connection to the recovery community.
- *Outcome:* Mark's commitment to community service not only strengthened his own sobriety but also inspired others on their paths to recovery. The sense of purpose and the positive impact on those he helped became integral to Mark's ongoing peace of mind.

3. Sophie's Bridge Across Generations:

- *Background:* Sophie, a retiree, felt a sense of emptiness after leaving her long-time career. She yearned for meaningful connections.
- *Community Service Experience:* Sophie joined a local program that paired seniors with young students for mentorship and academic support. She became actively involved in helping the younger generation navigate their educational journeys.
- *Transformation:* Through community service, Sophie discovered a new purpose in sharing her wisdom and experiences with younger individuals. The intergenerational connections brought her a sense of fulfillment and bridged the gap between different age groups.
- *Outcome:* Sophie's involvement in community service not only enriched the lives of the students she mentored but also brought her a profound sense of peace in knowing that she was making a positive impact on the future.

4. David's Reconnection with Society:

- *Background:* David, a military veteran, faced challenges adjusting to civilian life after his service. He experienced feelings of isolation and struggled with post-traumatic stress.
- *Community Service Experience:* David became involved in a local veterans' outreach program, offering support and companionship to fellow veterans facing similar challenges. He participated in community events that focused on veteran well-being.
- *Transformation:* Community service provided David with a renewed sense of camaraderie and belonging. Helping other veterans reintegrate into society became a therapeutic and purposeful mission for him.
- *Outcome:* Through his community service, David not only found peace in connecting with others who understood his experiences but also discovered a renewed sense of purpose in supporting fellow veterans on their journeys.

5. Emma's Empowerment through Education:

- *Background:* Emma, an educator, felt a desire to make a broader impact beyond the classroom. She sought a way to empower marginalized communities.
- *Community Service Experience:* Emma joined a literacy program that aimed to provide education to underserved communities. She dedicated her weekends to teaching reading and writing skills to children and adults who lacked access to formal education.

- *Transformation:* Emma's involvement in community service allowed her to witness the transformative power of education. She felt a deep sense of purpose in empowering individuals through knowledge and literacy.
- *Outcome:* Emma's commitment to community service not only positively impacted the lives of those she taught but also brought her a profound sense of peace, knowing that she was contributing to breaking the cycle of inequality through education.

Conclusion:

These anecdotes illustrate how individuals have found purpose and peace through community service. Engaging in acts of kindness and making a positive impact on others not only transforms the lives of those being served but also brings a profound sense of fulfillment and well-being to those who choose to give back to their communities.

In the exploration of the psychological effects of altruism, volunteerism, and community service on well-being, as well as the personal stories of individuals finding purpose and peace through these practices, several key findings emerged:

Psychological Effects of Altruism:

1. **Increased Happiness and Life Satisfaction:**
   - Engaging in acts of kindness and altruism is linked to higher levels of happiness and life satisfaction.
2. **Reduced Symptoms of Depression:**
   - Altruistic behaviors, such as helping others, have been associated with a decrease in symptoms of depression.
3. **Enhanced Emotional Well-Being:**
   - Altruistic acts contribute to enhanced emotional well-being, and there is evidence of a "helper's high" associated with altruism.
4. **Stress Reduction and Longevity:**
   - Experiencing positive emotions through altruistic acts may contribute to lower levels of inflammation, potentially impacting stress and longevity.
5. **Positive Impact on Relationships:**
   - Altruism fosters positive interpersonal relationships, creating a sense of connection and social bonding.
6. **Sense of Purpose and Meaning in Life:**
   - Engaging in altruistic behaviors contributes to an individual's sense of purpose and meaning in life.
7. **Positive Impact on Self-Esteem:**
   - Individuals who participate in altruistic activities, such as volunteering, report higher levels of self-esteem.

Personal Stories of Purpose and Peace:

1. **Rachel's Journey of Healing:**

    o   Through volunteering to support survivors of domestic violence, Rachel found purpose, healing, and a support system within the community.

2. **Mark's Path to Sobriety:**
    o   Volunteering at an addiction recovery center became a mission for Mark, providing him with renewed purpose and a deeper connection to the recovery community.
3. **Sophie's Bridge Across Generations:**
    o   Sophie's involvement in a mentorship program for seniors and students brought her a sense of fulfillment and peace through intergenerational connections.
4. **David's Reconnection with Society:**
    o   Engaging in a veterans' outreach program helped David find camaraderie, belonging, and a renewed sense of purpose in supporting fellow veterans.
5. **Emma's Empowerment through Education:**
    o   By dedicating her time to a literacy program, Emma discovered purpose and peace in empowering underserved communities through education.

Conclusion:

- Altruism, volunteerism, and community service have profound positive effects on psychological well-being, contributing to happiness, reduced depression, enhanced emotional well-being, and a sense of purpose. Personal stories highlight how individuals, through giving back, find healing, renewal, and a deeper connection to their communities, ultimately experiencing peace and fulfillment. The evidence suggests that the benefits of altruistic acts extend not only to those receiving help but also to the well-being of those offering kindness and support.

Call to Action: Embrace Altruism for Personal Fulfillment and Collective Well-Being

Dear Readers,

As we explore the profound impact of altruism, volunteerism, and community service on individual well-being and the stories of those who have found purpose and peace through these acts, we extend a heartfelt call to action. The evidence is clear: acts of kindness not only transform the lives of those you help but also enrich your own life in ways unimaginable.

Here's how you can embark on your journey of altruism and make a positive impact:

1. Discover Your Passion:

- Identify causes or issues that resonate with you. Whether it's supporting vulnerable populations, environmental conservation, or education, find a cause that aligns with your values.

2. Explore Volunteer Opportunities:

- Research local organizations and charities that address your chosen cause. Reach out to them and inquire about volunteer opportunities. Your time and skills can make a significant difference.

3. Start Small, Think Big:

- Begin with small acts of kindness in your community. Offer assistance to neighbors, participate in local clean-up efforts, or volunteer at a nearby shelter. Small gestures can create a ripple effect of positive change.

4. Engage in Random Acts of Kindness:

- Incorporate daily acts of kindness into your routine. Whether it's complimenting a colleague, helping a stranger, or expressing gratitude, these simple actions contribute to a more compassionate and connected world.

5. Share Your Skills:

- Consider how your unique talents and skills can benefit others. Offer to mentor, teach, or provide pro bono services to organizations in need.

6. Join Community Initiatives:

- Connect with local community initiatives and events. Participate in neighborhood projects, charity runs, or fundraising activities. Your involvement strengthens the bonds within your community.

7. Encourage Others to Join:

- Spread the message of altruism and encourage friends, family, and colleagues to join you on this journey. Collective efforts amplify the impact and create a culture of kindness.

8. Reflect on Your Journey:

- Take time to reflect on your experiences. Consider keeping a journal to document the positive moments, the lives touched, and the personal growth you've achieved through acts of altruism.

9. Share Your Story:

- If you've experienced the transformative power of altruism, share your story with others. Your narrative can inspire and motivate individuals to embrace kindness and make a difference.

10. Commit to Ongoing Growth:

- Altruism is a journey, not a destination. Commit to continuous personal growth through acts of kindness. Challenge yourself to explore new ways of contributing to the well-being of others and fostering a sense of community.

Embracing altruism is not only a gift to others but a gift to yourself. By fostering kindness and compassion, you contribute to a world where individuals find purpose, peace, and collective well-being.

Let your actions be the catalyst for positive change, and together, let's create a tapestry of kindness that binds us all.

Sincerely,

Donald V. Dunham

RESOURCES

Studies on mindfulness, well-being, and mental health

1. PubMed:

- Go to the PubMed website: PubMed.
- Use keywords related to your topics, such as "mindfulness," "well-being," or "mental health."
- Refine your search by adding specific terms or filters based on your book's focus.

2. PsycINFO:

- Access PsycINFO through your institution's library or a database subscription.
- Enter relevant keywords like "mindfulness," "well-being," or "mental health" in the search bar.
- Explore the results and use filters to narrow down your search based on publication type, date, etc.

3. Google Scholar:

- Visit Google Scholar at Google Scholar.
- Enter your keywords in the search bar.
- Explore the results and use the advanced search options to filter by time, citations, and more.

Example Search Queries:

- "Mindfulness and mental health intervention"
- "Well-being practices and psychological outcomes"
- "Effects of mindfulness on stress reduction"
- "Mindfulness-based therapies for anxiety"
- "Mindfulness and resilience in psychological well-being"

Tips:

- Use quotation marks for exact phrases.
- Experiment with different combinations of keywords.
- Check the publication date to ensure the information is current.
- Review the abstracts to gauge the relevance of the study.

Types of Resources to Consider:

Here is a curated list of well-reviewed and widely recognized books written by psychologists, mindfulness practitioners, and experts in the field of mindfulness, well-being, and mental health. These books cover a range of topics, from the science behind mindfulness to practical guides for achieving inner peace:

1. "The Miracle of Mindfulness" by Thich Nhat Hanh

- *Author:* Thich Nhat Hanh, Zen master and renowned mindfulness teacher
- *Overview:* A classic guide on mindfulness meditation, offering practical techniques to bring mindfulness into everyday life.

2. "Wherever You Go, There You Are" by Jon Kabat-Zinn

- *Author:* Jon Kabat-Zinn, founder of the Mindfulness-Based Stress Reduction (MBSR) program
- *Overview:* A guide to mindfulness meditation, emphasizing the importance of being present and cultivating awareness in each moment.

3. "The Untethered Soul: The Journey Beyond Yourself" by Michael A. Singer

- *Author:* Michael A. Singer, spiritual teacher and author
- *Overview:* Explores the concept of self and the transformative power of mindfulness to achieve inner freedom.

4. "Radical Acceptance: Embracing Your Life With the Heart of a Buddha" by Tara Brach

- *Author:* Tara Brach, clinical psychologist and mindfulness teacher
- *Overview:* Integrates mindfulness and self-compassion, offering guidance on accepting ourselves and our lives with compassion.

5. "Mindset: The New Psychology of Success" by Carol S. Dweck

- *Author:* Carol S. Dweck, psychologist and motivation researcher
- *Overview:* Explores the concept of mindset and how it shapes success, happiness, and fulfillment.

6. "The Power of Now: A Guide to Spiritual Enlightenment" by Eckhart Tolle

- *Author:* Eckhart Tolle, spiritual teacher and author
- *Overview:* Emphasizes the importance of living in the present moment and transcending the ego for spiritual awakening.

7. "Man's Search for Meaning" by Viktor E. Frankl

- *Author:* Viktor E. Frankl, psychiatrist and Holocaust survivor
- *Overview:* A profound exploration of finding meaning and purpose in life, even in the face of suffering.

8. "The Happiness Hypothesis: Finding Modern Truth in Ancient Wisdom" by Jonathan Haidt

- *Author:* Jonathan Haidt, psychologist and happiness researcher
- *Overview:* Blends ancient wisdom with modern science to explore the factors that contribute to happiness.

9. "Full Catastrophe Living: Using the Wisdom of Your Body and Mind to Face Stress, Pain, and Illness" by Jon Kabat-Zinn

- *Author:* Jon Kabat-Zinn, founder of the Mindfulness-Based Stress Reduction (MBSR) program
- *Overview:* Provides a comprehensive guide to using mindfulness to cope with stress, pain, and illness.

10. "The Body Keeps the Score: Brain, Mind, and Body in the Healing of Trauma" by Bessel van der Kolk

- *Author:* Bessel van der Kolk, psychiatrist and trauma expert
- *Overview:* Explores the impact of trauma on the body and mind, offering insights into healing through mindfulness.

These books offer a diverse perspective on mindfulness, well-being, and mental health, and they are highly recommended by both readers and experts in the field.

Popular mindfulness apps that offer guided meditations and mindfulness exercises, such as Headspace, Calm, or Insight Timer.

1. Headspace

- *Overview:* Headspace is known for its user-friendly interface and a variety of guided meditations. It covers topics like stress reduction, sleep, and focus. The app also offers mindfulness exercises for kids.
- *Availability:* Headspace

2. Calm

- *Overview:* Calm is recognized for its soothing nature sounds, guided meditations, and sleep stories. It provides a wide range of meditation sessions, including those focused on anxiety relief and gratitude.
- *Availability:* Calm

3. Insight Timer

- *Overview:* Insight Timer is a diverse meditation app with a large library of guided sessions led by different teachers. It includes meditations for sleep, stress reduction, and personal growth.
- *Availability:* Insight Timer

4. 10% Happier

- *Overview:* Developed by journalist Dan Harris, 10% Happier offers mindfulness meditations designed for skeptics. It includes talks and courses on understanding the science behind meditation.
- *Availability:* 10% Happier

5. Simple Habit

- *Overview:* Simple Habit is designed for busy lifestyles, offering short guided meditations tailored to specific situations like commuting, work breaks, and stress relief.
- *Availability:* Simple Habit

6. Aura

- *Overview:* Aura provides personalized mindfulness exercises based on users' moods and preferences. It includes guided meditations, nature sounds, and life coaching sessions.
- *Availability:* Aura

7. Stop, Breathe & Think

- *Overview:* This app encourages users to check in with their emotions before suggesting personalized mindfulness exercises. It offers guided meditations, breathing exercises, and yoga sessions.
- *Availability:* Stop, Breathe & Think

8. Smiling Mind

- *Overview:* Smiling Mind is designed for all age groups and includes mindfulness programs for individuals, workplaces, and schools. It focuses on building resilience and promoting well-being.
- *Availability:* Smiling Mind

9. Breathe

- *Overview:* Breethe offers guided meditations, calming music, and sleep stories. It has programs for stress reduction, improved sleep, and overall well-being.
- *Availability:* Breethe

10. Mindfulness Daily

- *Overview:* Mindfulness Daily provides daily mindfulness exercises, including guided meditations and reflections. It aims to make mindfulness a habit with short, daily practices.
- *Availability:* Mindfulness Daily

Before choosing an app, consider your preferences, the features offered, and the specific areas of mindfulness and well-being that are important to you. Many apps offer free trials, so you can explore and find the one that best suits your needs.

How to find scholarly articles on the psychological and physiological effects of mindfulness and inner peace. Here are steps you can take:

1. PubMed:

- Visit PubMed.
- In the search bar, enter keywords such as "mindfulness," "inner peace," "psychological effects," and "physiological effects."
- Use filters on the left side to refine your search by article type, publication date, and more.

2. Google Scholar:

- Go to Google Scholar.
- Enter your keywords in the search bar.
- Review the search results and use advanced search options for more specific queries.

3. PsycINFO:

- Access PsycINFO through your institution's library or a database subscription.
- Enter relevant keywords in the search bar.
- Refine your search using the available filters.

4. ResearchGate:

- Visit ResearchGate.
- Enter your keywords in the search bar to find academic papers shared by researchers.

- Explore academic journals related to psychology, mindfulness, and well-being.
- Journals such as "Mindfulness," "Journal of Positive Psychology," and "Psychosomatic Medicine" often feature relevant articles.

6. University Repositories:

- Check university repositories for the latest research papers and theses on mindfulness and inner peace.
- Explore repositories like ProQuest Dissertations & Theses and individual university databases.

7. Citations in Existing Papers:

- Review the references and citations in existing papers or books related to mindfulness. This can lead you to foundational studies.

Example Search Queries:

- "Mindfulness and physiological effects"
- "Psychological impact of inner peace"
- "Neuroscience of mindfulness"
- "Mindfulness-based interventions and well-being"

Tips:

- Use specific and relevant keywords for more accurate results.
- Pay attention to the publication date to ensure the information is current.
- Consider articles from reputable journals and authors.

By using these search strategies, you should be able to find academic papers that delve into the psychological and physiological effects of mindfulness and inner peace. Always ensure that you have access to the full text of the papers through your institution's library or other legitimate means.

Online courses on platforms like Coursera, edX, and Udemy offer a convenient way to explore mindfulness, stress reduction, and achieving inner peace. Here are some recommended courses:

Coursera:

1. **Mindfulness and Well-being:**
   - *Offered by:* Monash University
   - *Overview:* Explore the science and practice of mindfulness, learning techniques to reduce stress and enhance well-being.
2. **Mindfulness-Based Stress Reduction (MBSR):**
   - *Offered by:* University of California, San Diego

- o *Overview:* Based on the renowned MBSR program, this course teaches mindfulness practices for stress reduction.
3. <u>The Science of Happiness:</u>
     - o *Offered by:* Yale University
     - o *Overview:* Explores the science behind happiness, stress reduction, and strategies for improving well-being.
4. <u>Mind Control: Managing Your Mental Health During COVID-19:</u>
     - o *Offered by:* University of Toronto
     - o *Overview:* Focuses on managing mental health during challenging times, incorporating mindfulness and stress reduction techniques.

edX:

1. <u>Introduction to Mindfulness:</u>
     - o *Offered by:* University of Oxford
     - o *Overview:* A professional certificate program introducing the principles and practices of mindfulness.
2. <u>Foundations of Positive Psychology:</u>
     - o *Offered by:* University of California, Berkeley
     - o *Overview:* Explores the science of happiness and well-being, incorporating mindfulness practices.
3. <u>Stress Management and Mindfulness in the Workplace:</u>
     - o *Offered by:* University of California, Irvine
     - o *Overview:* Designed for stress reduction and promoting well-being in the workplace.

Udemy:

1. <u>Mindfulness Practitioner Course (Beginner to Advanced):</u>
     - o *Instructor:* Kain Ramsay
     - o *Overview:* A comprehensive course covering mindfulness techniques for practitioners at all levels.
2. <u>Stress Management: A Guide to Overcoming Stress:</u>
     - o *Instructor:* Joeel & Natalie Rivera
     - o *Overview:* Practical strategies for managing and reducing stress, including mindfulness practices.
3. <u>The Science of Happiness: Positive Psychology Practices:</u>
     - o *Instructor:* Kain Ramsay
     - o *Overview:* Focuses on positive psychology and mindfulness for increased happiness.

Remember to check reviews, course content, and instructor credentials before enrolling in any course. Additionally, these platforms often offer discounts, so keep an eye out for promotions that may make the courses more accessible.

Some documentaries and videos on mindfulness practices, the science behind meditation, and personal stories of transformation. You can find these on popular streaming platforms, YouTube, or through official websites. Please use the titles as search queries on your preferred platform. Here are some recommendations:

Documentaries:

1. **"Free the Mind"**
   - *Overview:* Explores the use of mindfulness and meditation to address trauma, particularly in military veterans.
2. **"The Connection: Mind Your Body"**
   - *Overview:* Investigates the link between mind and body, featuring experts discussing the impact of mindfulness on health.
3. **"Walk With Me"**
   - *Overview:* Takes viewers into the world of mindfulness with the renowned Thich Nhat Hanh and his community.
4. **"Innsaei: The Power of Intuition"**
   - *Overview:* Explores mindfulness and intuition, discussing their role in personal and societal well-being.
5. **"On Meditation"**
   - *Overview:* A series of short films capturing the diverse experiences and benefits of meditation.

Videos:

1. **"The Science of Mindfulness" (TEDx Talk by Dr. Dan Siegel)**
   - *Overview:* Dr. Dan Siegel discusses the scientific understanding of mindfulness and its impact on the brain.
2. **"How Meditation Can Reshape Our Brains" (TED Talk by Sara Lazar)**
   - *Overview:* Neuroscientist Sara Lazar explains the positive effects of meditation on brain structure.
3. **"Mindfulness in the Digital Age" (Talk by Jon Kabat-Zinn)**
   - *Overview:* Jon Kabat-Zinn, a pioneer in the field of mindfulness, discusses its relevance in our digital age.
4. **"The Power of Vulnerability" (TED Talk by Brené Brown)**
   - *Overview:* While not directly about mindfulness, Brené Brown's talk explores the importance of vulnerability, a key aspect of mindfulness.
5. **"Meditation: Changing Your Brain for a Better You" (National Geographic)**
   - *Overview:* Examines the neuroscience behind meditation and its impact on the brain.

YouTube Channels:

1. **Mindful.org**
   - *Overview:* Mindful.org offers a variety of videos on mindfulness practices, guided meditations, and expert interviews.

2. **The Chopra Well**
   o *Overview:* Deepak Chopra's YouTube channel includes videos on meditation, well-being, and personal transformation.
3. **Thich Nhat Hanh Foundation**
   o *Overview:* Features videos of teachings by Thich Nhat Hanh, a renowned Buddhist monk and mindfulness teacher.
4. **Headspace**
   o *Overview:* The Headspace YouTube channel includes guided meditations, animations, and discussions on mindfulness.

Remember to use these titles as search queries on your preferred platforms to find the content easily. Additionally, some documentaries may be available on streaming services or official websites of the filmmakers.

Podcasts are a great way to explore discussions on mindfulness, mental health, and finding peace. Here are some recommendations that you can find on popular podcast platforms like Spotify or Apple Podcasts:

1. "The Mindful Kind"

- *Host:* Rachael Kable
- *Overview:* A podcast that covers mindfulness, stress reduction, and living a more intentional life. Rachael provides practical tips and interviews experts in the field.

2. "The Daily Meditation Podcast"

- *Host:* Mary Meckley
- *Overview:* Offers daily guided meditations and discussions on various aspects of meditation, mindfulness, and stress reduction.

3. "10% Happier with Dan Harris"

- *Host:* Dan Harris
- *Overview:* ABC News anchor Dan Harris explores mindfulness with various experts, discussing practical tips and personal stories of transformation.

4. "The Calm Collective"

- *Host:* Cassandra Eldridge
- *Overview:* Explores topics related to self-care, mindfulness, and finding calm in the midst of a busy life. Features interviews with wellness experts.

5. "The Minimalists Podcast"

- *Hosts:* Joshua Fields Millburn and Ryan Nicodemus

- *Overview:* While not solely focused on mindfulness, this podcast explores minimalism as a tool for living a more intentional and meaningful life.

6. "Happier with Gretchen Rubin"

- *Hosts:* Gretchen Rubin and Elizabeth Craft
- *Overview:* Gretchen Rubin, a happiness expert, discusses practical strategies for living a happier life, often touching on mindfulness and well-being.

7. "Tara Brach"

- *Host:* Tara Brach
- *Overview:* Tara Brach, a psychologist and meditation teacher, shares talks and guided meditations that blend psychology, mindfulness, and spirituality.

8. "The School of Greatness"

- *Host:* Lewis Howes
- *Overview:* While covering a range of topics, Lewis Howes often explores personal development, mindfulness, and well-being with various guests.

9. "The Goop Podcast"

- *Host:* Gwyneth Paltrow
- *Overview:* Explores topics related to health, wellness, and personal growth, often featuring discussions on mindfulness and finding balance.

10. "The Dharma Seed Podcast"

- *Overview:* Offers talks and guided meditations by various meditation teachers and practitioners, providing a wealth of insights into mindfulness and Buddhist teachings.

Remember to check the latest episodes and reviews to ensure that the content aligns with your interests and preferences. These podcasts can be found on major podcast platforms like Spotify, Apple Podcasts, or their respective websites.

Here are links to some TED Talks that touch upon topics related to well-being, mindfulness, and achieving peace. You can watch these talks on the official TED website or on YouTube:

1. "All it Takes is 10 Mindful Minutes" by Andy Puddicombe

- *Overview:* Andy Puddicombe, co-founder of Headspace, talks about the transformative power of taking just 10 minutes a day to be mindful.

2. "The Power of Vulnerability" by Brené Brown

- *Overview:* Brené Brown explores the connection between vulnerability, courage, and well-being, emphasizing the importance of embracing our imperfections.

3. "The Art of Stillness" by Pico Iyer

- *Overview:* Pico Iyer discusses the value of stillness and mindfulness in our fast-paced world, exploring how moments of quiet can lead to greater clarity.

4. "How to Make Stress Your Friend" by Kelly McGonigal

- *Overview:* Kelly McGonigal reframes how we view stress, presenting it as a positive force that can enhance resilience and well-being.

5. "The Habits of Happiness" by Matthieu Ricard

- *Overview:* Matthieu Ricard, a Buddhist monk and happiness researcher, shares insights on cultivating happiness through habits and mindfulness.

6. "The Surprising Science of Happiness" by Dan Gilbert

- *Overview:* Dan Gilbert explores the science of happiness, challenging common beliefs about what makes us happy and fulfilled.

7. "The Hidden Influence of Social Networks" by Nicholas Christakis

- *Overview:* Nicholas Christakis discusses the impact of social networks on well-being, highlighting the interconnected nature of human relationships.

8. "What Makes a Good Life? Lessons from the Longest Study on Happiness" by Robert Waldinger

- *Overview:* Robert Waldinger shares insights from the longest-running study on happiness, emphasizing the importance of quality relationships for well-being.

9. "The Benefits of Mindfulness and Meditation" by Danny Penman

- *Overview:* Danny Penman discusses the scientific benefits of mindfulness and meditation, exploring their impact on mental health and well-being.

10. "How to Stay Calm When You Know You'll be Stressed" by Daniel Levitin

- *Overview:* Daniel Levitin shares strategies for staying calm in stressful situations, drawing on neuroscience and mindfulness.

Feel free to explore these talks to gain valuable insights into mindfulness, well-being, and achieving peace. You can access them directly on the TED website or through the provided links.

Websites of reputable organizations dedicated to mindfulness and well-being, such as the Mindful Awareness Research Center (MARC) or the Center for Mindful Self-Compassion.

1. Mindful Awareness Research Center (MARC)

- *Overview:* MARC at UCLA is dedicated to researching and promoting mindfulness practices. Their website offers resources, guided meditations, and information on mindfulness programs.

2. Center for Mindful Self-Compassion

- *Overview:* The Center for Mindful Self-Compassion provides resources and training related to self-compassion. Their website includes information on MSC courses, workshops, and events.

3. Mindfulness-Based Stress Reduction (MBSR)

- *Overview:* Mindful Living Programs offers information and resources on Mindfulness-Based Stress Reduction (MBSR), including courses and retreats.

4. Greater Good Science Center

- *Overview:* Based at UC Berkeley, the Greater Good Science Center offers resources on the science of well-being, including practices related to mindfulness and compassion.

5. The Mindfulness Initiative

- *Overview:* The Mindfulness Initiative works to promote the use of mindfulness in policy and societal well-being. Their website includes reports, resources, and events.

6. Mindfulness in Schools Project (MiSP)

- *Overview:* MiSP is dedicated to bringing mindfulness to education. Their website provides resources for educators, parents, and students.

7. Mind and Life Institute

- *Overview:* The Mind and Life Institute fosters dialogue and research between the sciences and contemplative wisdom. Their website includes resources, events, and publications.

8. The Center for Contemplative Mind in Society

- *Overview:* The Center for Contemplative Mind in Society promotes contemplative practices in higher education. Their website offers resources and programs.

9. The Oxford Mindfulness Centre

- *Overview:* Based at the University of Oxford, this center conducts research and offers training in mindfulness. Their website provides information on courses and resources.

10. Association for Mindfulness in Education

- *Overview:* The Association for Mindfulness in Education provides resources and training for educators interested in incorporating mindfulness into schools.

Encourage readers to explore these websites for a wealth of information, courses, and resources related to mindfulness, well-being, and mental health. Each organization has its unique focus and offerings, contributing to the broader field of mindfulness.

Joining online forums and communities can be a valuable way for individuals to share experiences, ask questions, and find support on their mindfulness journey. Here are some platforms and forums where discussions on mindfulness and finding peace are active:

1. r/Mindfulness on Reddit

- *Overview:* A Reddit community dedicated to discussions on mindfulness, meditation, and related topics. Members share experiences, resources, and support.

2. r/Meditation on Reddit

- *Overview:* While not exclusively focused on mindfulness, this Reddit community covers a broad range of meditation practices. Members often share insights and experiences.

3. Insight Timer Community

- *Overview:* Insight Timer, a meditation app, has a vibrant online community where users discuss their meditation experiences, share tips, and offer support.

4. Wildmind Buddhist Meditation Forum

- *Overview:* This forum is dedicated to discussions on Buddhist meditation, mindfulness, and related practices. It's a supportive community for those interested in Buddhist teachings.

5. Dharma Overground Forum

- *Overview:* An online community discussing various meditation practices and experiences. It provides a platform for in-depth discussions on mindfulness and related topics.

6. Elephant Journal Community

- *Overview:* Elephant Journal hosts a community where members share personal stories, articles, and insights related to mindfulness, well-being, and personal growth.

7. Mindful.org Community

- *Overview:* Mindful.org has a community section where individuals can connect, share their mindfulness experiences, and participate in discussions on well-being.

8. Zen Habits Forum

- *Overview:* Zen Habits, a popular blog on mindfulness and simplicity, has an active forum where members discuss mindfulness practices and personal development.

9. The Quiet Place Community

- *Overview:* The Quiet Place Project hosts a community for individuals to share moments of calm, mindfulness practices, and reflections on finding peace.

10. Sangha Online

- *Overview:* Sangha Online is a platform for practitioners of mindfulness and meditation to connect, share experiences, and engage in discussions.

Creating a peaceful atmosphere at home often involves incorporating products that contribute to relaxation, comfort, and tranquility. Here's a list of companies that offer products designed to enhance the peaceful ambiance of the home:

1. **Yankee Candle:**
   - *Products:* Scented candles, reed diffusers, and home fragrance solutions.
2. **Brooklinen:**
   - *Products:* High-quality bedding and home essentials for a cozy and peaceful bedroom.
3. **MUJI:**
   - *Products:* Minimalist and calming home goods, including furniture, bedding, and accessories.
4. **Saje Natural Wellness:**
   - *Products:* Essential oils, diffusers, and wellness products to promote relaxation.
5. **The White Company:**
   - *Products:* Elegant and serene home furnishings, bedding, and candles.
6. **Boll & Branch:**
   - *Products:* Organic and sustainable bedding and bath linens.

7. <u>Manduka</u>:
   - *Products:* Yoga mats, props, and accessories for creating a serene yoga and meditation space.
8. <u>Gravity Blankets</u>:
   - *Products:* Weighted blankets designed to promote relaxation and improve sleep quality.
9. <u>Himalayan Salt Shop</u>:
   - *Products:* Himalayan salt lamps and other salt-based products for a calming ambiance.
10. <u>Parachute Home</u>:
    - *Products:* Thoughtfully designed bedding, bath linens, and home essentials.
11. <u>Essentia</u>:
    - *Products:* Natural and organic mattresses and sleep accessories.
12. <u>Serena & Lily</u>:
    - *Products:* Coastal-inspired home decor and furnishings for a relaxed atmosphere.
13. <u>Aromatech</u>:
    - *Products:* Commercial-grade aroma diffusers and essential oils for home fragrance.
14. <u>Urban Outfitters Home</u>:
    - *Products:* Eclectic and bohemian home decor items for a unique and calming space.
15. <u>Lunya</u>:
    - *Products:* Comfortable and stylish sleepwear designed for a restful night's sleep.

When exploring products from these companies, individuals can find items that suit their preferences and contribute to a peaceful and harmonious home environment

Companies that teach ways to achieve peace in life

Many companies and organizations offer teachings, courses, and resources to help individuals achieve peace in their lives. Here's a list of companies and platforms that focus on providing guidance, tools, and insights for finding inner peace:

1. <u>Headspace</u>:
   - *Overview:* Headspace offers guided meditations, mindfulness exercises, and courses to promote mental well-being and peace of mind.
2. <u>Calm</u>:
   - *Overview:* Calm is a meditation app that provides guided meditations, sleep stories, and calming music to help users achieve relaxation and peace.
3. <u>The Chopra Center</u>:
   - *Overview:* Founded by Deepak Chopra, The Chopra Center offers programs and resources focused on meditation, wellness, and spiritual growth.
4. <u>Mindvalley</u>:
   - *Overview:* Mindvalley offers personal development courses covering various aspects of life, including meditation and mindfulness for a more fulfilling and peaceful existence.
5. <u>Sounds True</u>:

- o *Overview:* Sounds True provides courses, books, and resources on spirituality, mindfulness, and personal growth to support individuals on their journey to peace.
6. **Insight Timer:**
    - o *Overview:* Insight Timer is a meditation app with a vast library of guided meditations, courses, and talks led by meditation teachers worldwide.
7. **Shambhala Publications:**
    - o *Overview:* Shambhala Publications offers books and resources on mindfulness, meditation, and Eastern philosophy to foster peace and well-being.
8. **Mindful Schools:**
    - o *Overview:* Mindful Schools provides training and resources for educators, parents, and individuals interested in bringing mindfulness to schools and communities.
9. **Hay House:**
    - o *Overview:* Hay House publishes books, courses, and events on spiritual growth, self-help, and mindfulness, featuring renowned authors and teachers.
10. **The Art of Living:**
    - o *Overview:* The Art of Living offers programs on yoga, meditation, and holistic well-being, emphasizing the importance of a peaceful and stress-free life.
11. **The Tapping Solution:**
    - o *Overview:* The Tapping Solution focuses on Emotional Freedom Techniques (EFT), offering resources and courses to address stress and achieve emotional peace.
12. **Buddha Groove:**
    - o *Overview:* Buddha Groove offers mindful living products, including meditation tools, jewelry, and decor, to inspire a peaceful lifestyle.
13. **Mind Body Green:**
    - o *Overview:* Mind Body Green provides articles, courses, and resources on holistic wellness, mindfulness, and lifestyle practices for a balanced life.
14. **Omega Institute:**
    - o *Overview:* Omega Institute offers workshops, retreats, and online courses covering spiritual growth, mindfulness, and personal development.
15. **DailyOM:**
    - o *Overview:* DailyOM offers online courses on various topics, including meditation, self-discovery, and holistic well-being.

These companies provide a range of teachings and resources to support individuals in their journey towards inner peace and well-being. It's advisable for individuals to explore these platforms, courses, and teachings to find what resonates best with their personal preferences and goals.

www.ingramcontent.com/pod-product-compliance
Lightning Source LLC
Chambersburg PA
CBHW081236130726
47997CB00009B/2896